# Minding your own Business

# Minding your own Business

A COMMON SENSE GUIDE TO HOME MANAGEMENT AND INDUSTRY.

## Raymond & Dorothy Moore

Wolgemuth & Hyatt, Publishers, Inc.
Brentwood, Tennessee

The mission of Wolgemuth & Hyatt, Publishers, Inc. is to publish and distribute books that lead individuals toward:

- A personal faith in the one true God: Father, Son, and Holy Spirit;

- A lifestyle of practical discipleship; and

- A worldview that is consistent with the historic, Christian faith.

Moreover, the Company endeavors to accomplish this mission at a reasonable profit and in a manner which glorifies God and serves His Kingdom.

Wolgemuth & Hyatt, Publishers, Inc.
1749 Mallory Lane, Suite 110
Brentwood, Tennessee 37027

**Library of Congress Cataloging-in-Publication Data**

Moore, Raymond S.
    Minding your own business : a common sense guide to home
management and industry / Raymond and Dorothy Moore.
        p.   cm.
    Includes bibliographical references.
    ISBN 1-56121-008-0
    1. Home-based businesses.   I. Moore, Dorothy N.   II. Title.
HD2333.M66   1990
    658'.041—dc20

                                                        90-44989
                                                            CIP

To our fathers and mothers
who understood the value
of the work ethic and
had the patience and creativity
to follow through

# CONTENTS

# ACKNOWLEDGMENTS

This book was put together by a couple of frankly old-fashioned authors with the help of a lot of young parents with old-fashioned values . . . and some very special experiences. We won't repeat their names here—for there are over a hundred—who embrace the work ethic and selfless service as a way of life. When you see their names in the book, let them remind you that they are first honored in this acknowledgment. We can only recall losing one name—"L. G." in Tennessee—about whom you will read in chapter 11. This housewife and mother both wrote and phoned us, and Dorothy wrote about her in a bi-monthly newsletter. We hope that she finds us, for her story is one of the clearest examples of an almost hopeless "unemployed" housewife who feared starting a business, yet by following the very simple formula in this book quickly became a happy and successful businesswoman.

There are several whom we should mention, however, who helped directly or encouraged us in this project. Chapter 3 is primarily graced with the common sense of Larry Burkett, well-known author and financial counselor. Organizer Pat Burris and *The Desert Sun* gave us a boost in chapter 8, and *Family Circle* magazine gave us much of chapter 15.

Overall, we are grateful to the distinguished panel who have critiqued our manuscript in galley, such as Gary Bauer of the Family Research Council of America, Tony Campolo of Eastern College, Barrie Lyons of Concerned Women for America, Marlin and Mary Maddoux of *Point of View*, Earl McGrath, formerly of Columbia University and U.S. Commissioner of Education, Jerry Regier of the U.S. Department of Justice, Phyllis Schafly of *Eagle Forum,* and Robert Strom of the Office for Parent Development International and Arizona State University.

Our purpose here is to help not only those families who need money but much more importantly, those who *remedially* need self-respect and relief from alcohol, drugs, and family separation, and who *preventively* are determined to rear principled, secure, and creative children like Pearl Buck, Andrew Carnegie, George Washington Carver, Thomas Edison, Sara Hale, Abraham Lincoln, Margaret Mead, Sir Isaac Newton, Orville and Wilbur Wright, all of whom by their examples would have endorsed the methods and goals of this book. Not until America adopts these old-but-proven principles and methods, and earns the confidence they bring, will our nation renew its moral and creative strength.

# PROLOGUE

# ON BECOMING A HOME MANAGEMENT EXPERT

R unning a family is much like running a business: No matter how wonderful and warm your family, if you don't use your heads, take counsel, and work together, you may eventually suffer separately. That happened in my family, and we tell that story in chapter 1.

In our fifty-two years of family counseling, we have found thousands of parents and children struggling to keep alive, stay together, and save their homes, while others nearby, with fewer basic assets, thrive. In this book we give you hundreds of stories and ideas to show how families cooperate to the advantage of every member and of society. What if there is a little friction or competition within your family? As in any business, so in the family, simple competition thrives with cooperation, in sharp contrast with vicious rivalry we have seen in both the workplace and the family when the goal of cooperation is absent. We offer you something better than the selfishness and vanity which so deftly distort relationships crucial to sound management at home or anywhere.

*1*

## Expedience and Principle

Such principles and practices are universal. American management consultant Peter Drucker expresses concern about the greed he sees in much of industry, particularly these days in the giant "transnational economies" (TE) which have already altered the balance in our world exchange and virtually control the finances of nations. The aim of these giant TEs (now even larger than the once-feared monopolies of generations ago) is to drive the competitor out of the market altogether rather than to let it survive. Similarly vested business and state forces are almost identically targeting the family.

The same spirit brought on by the denial of principle and respect was identified by philosopher Victor Frankl from his experiences under Adolf Hitler before and during World War II and the Holocaust. In either business or family economics, expediency— the thinking of convenience—overtakes principle and its truths when our greedy purses reach out to satisfy our own wants. Recently we have reached out to other nations, not to help them as we once did under the Marshall Plan after World War II, but to take advantage of their low pay scales, suffering economies, and their discipline of poverty with which they underbid American competition. This is understood by few, yet it has profound meaning for all of us in industry and home.

To further clarify and to apply this lesson: A friend of ours recently shamed us for driving a foreign car—in this case a used Swedish Saab which one of our board members gave to the Moore Foundation. Our critical friend urged us to "Buy American," and we generally agree. He points out with his tongue rolling in his cheeks, that he drives an *American* car, a 1989 Pontiac Le Mans. What he didn't know was that his car was designed in West Germany, has an Australian-made engine (or South Korean), a transmission from Canada or the U.S., a radio from Singapore, sheet metal from Japan, tires and electrical wiring and battery made in South Korea, fuel pump from America, ad infinitum.

Just as Dr. Drucker urges regional consortiums, cooperative groups, which balance or counter TEs and support national or regional economies and keep them alive in a world economy, so we urge cooperation within and among families. Just as Victor Frankl urges our nation to courageously adhere to principle over expediency, (lest we fall again into pre-Hitlerian indifference which brought Dr. Frankl torture during World War II), so we urge the same principles and practices within the family, lest we find ourselves surrendering to forces eagerly working against us. If our families don't work together within our communities, our society will not long survive.

You will see something of the specific ways we can do this in chapter 4 on waste and in chapter 5 on recycling. Where there is waste, costs go up for all; where people don't take care of their homes, neighborhoods depreciate; where we don't take care of our bodies, we incur higher health costs; where we drink and drive, we take lives and add many billions of dollars and barrels of tears to our economy.

Communities, school districts, and home school support groups offer opportunities for getting together in home industries for production or manufacture and marketing. Two or three families can make wooden toys, with children over age sixteen running the power tools and younger children sanding, assembling, packaging, and shipping. With common marketing objectives and love and respect for each other, we become more efficient.

In higher education, North Carolina's Duke and Oregon's Willamette Universities offer a shining example: Duke welcomes fourth-year students from Willamette to its senior forestry courses, yet lets Willamette grant the A.B. degree. Then Duke gives the Willamette seniors a masters degree in forestry after an additional year at Duke. Such cooperation guarantees great quality while saving millions of dollars incurred with duplicate programs.

Sometimes we suffer from ignorance, misinformation, or indifference as well as greed. A few months ago I needed to find a jeweler who could treat my old International self-winding wristwatch (no bother with batteries) which had suddenly had a heart attack after more than thirty-five years of almost perfect health. Jeweler after jeweler said no one in America could heal it, although one of them referred me to an old Swiss jeweler in a fashionable area of town, inferring that he might be outlandishly expensive and suggesting that it would be wise to send the watch to the factory at Schauffhausen, Switzerland, where it was made and would cost at least several hundred dollars for treatment.

In desperation I sent the watch to International's New York office for an estimate. They agreed that the very fine old watch was on its deathbed, and advised that if the factory could revive it at all, the bill might be five hundred dollars or more. I was ready to lay the watch in a casket on my bedside stand when I thought again about that old Swiss jeweler—who in a few weeks operated and healed it . . . for only sixty dollars.

Dorothy and I have well over fifty years of home and institutional management and considerably more than sixty years of successful work experience as laborers, supervisors, teachers, or administrators. We are certain that there is no simpler and sounder solution to standard family problems of both parents and children, and no better route to happiness, than a realistic family management and work program based on mutual respect, cooperation, and a willingness to venture—whether it be an old jeweler or starting a new family industry. If you have any doubts about the possibilities, please wait until you give the many stories in this book a fair reading.

## The Lessons of the Depression

Those who went through the Great Depression following the collapse of Wall Street in 1929 will understand the next paragraph or two. After an almost wild period of prosperity, Americans found themselves living from hand to mouth. Families, once careless, had to pull together; everyone pulled his share of the load, from the small child to grandpas and grandmas. But fifteen to twenty years later, when the kids of the Depression began to have their own offspring, they made up their minds that "our kids are not going to suffer like we did." And that was the mistake of the century.

Children who were not called on to sacrifice did not learn the art of manners and respect. Greed replaced grace, and rivalry destroyed the old-fashioned spirit of family cooperation. In the prosperity of still another generation that followed World War II, the high-spirited conquerors multiplied their folly by indulging their own children and begat a variety of indolent and indigent cultures which threw manners, self-respect, and cooperation even further out the window.

Instead of work, we gave our children and grandchildren play. Instead of manual skills, we provided amusements. Instead of manners, we offered allowances which generated ingratitude more than appreciation. Those few who remembered the lessons of the Great Depression and the treasures of cooperation, thoughtfulness, and the work ethic, were the exception. But they were the ones who brought up self-controlled, happy children. For the work ethic, well understood and practiced, is the finest disciplinary tool that parents can use to shape and build a strong, noble, productive, and compassionate family and to reshape those who are inclined to rebel. When we become realistic about this ethic, we will no longer have a labor pool of late and lazy, indifferent and apathetic youth who think the world owes them a living, just because their parents have always given it to them.

## The Focus of This Book

In seminars and counseling sessions, by telephone and letter, thousands of you have for years been asking that we share more of our home and institutional management and industry ideas which have blessed us now for well over fifty years. Some reviewers said before it was published that this is an idea book. We hope so, but more than that, it is an experience book. We include only ideas and solutions which have been proven in practice. With reasonable care it will help almost any person or family become reasonably efficient in home management and comfortable in home businesses.

It is a fact that our family has long been financially independent, and that every institution—school system, college, university, or foundation—whose management we've shared has prospered. This is not because we are brilliant, but rather that we sought advisors who were experienced and wise—who had some of the elements of the common sense that permeates Peter Drucker's every paragraph and the compassion reflected in Victor Frankl's every word.

This book is unique in its focus on both parents and children and its inclusion of both home management and industries. We tried to give it a coverage, with listings or stories on more than five hundred industries and services, that gives it special value. We have also, as usual, saturated it with stories, poignant ones, we believe.

If you read this book, you are likely one of several characters:

- Someone who has gone through financial fires or been much too close to them;

- A common-sense type who cherishes practical experience without making the same mistakes others have;

- Just a book worm or a curiosity freak.

We, your authors, are all three. Whatever *you* are, we hope you find the ideas workable. All will not apply to your family, but, whether you are rich or poor or in between and regardless of color or creed, some ideas can and will take some risk out of your future.

So we write to you as one man's family who has been through the mill, as well as the hundreds of students, counselees, officials, and friends who shared their problems and successes with us. These principles and methods have succeeded significantly in both institutions and homes. To this day, we don't know of any who tried them fully and persistently who haven't done reasonably well, and who have not in most cases flourished.

As some of you read, we can hear you thinking or commenting that some of these pointers are "too penny-pinching frugal to be bothered with." Some have even applied the words "stingy" or "niggardly" to individuals who have practiced some of these principles and methods. You won't catch us counseling extreme changes. But we suggest that those who are leaning more to frugality tend usually to be more quality-bound and happier and more selfless in the long run; while those who accuse of stinginess and niggardliness are often among the unfortunates whose careless or prodigal ways have driven them close to poverty's cliffs.

There is no perfect order for this book in chapter sequence or book sections. We placed Part I on home management before industries because it will help you make decisions in building your home industry if you have a few simple but sound ideas about management. If you are already a mature manager, you may appreciate Part II even more. But we are still learning and assume that you are, too. Otherwise you—and we—could rationalize almost any order for the chapters.

At times we deliberately take a long term view where we suggest sharing management with others. An example is recycling. This is a community idea on which we have plenty of information these days, yet because of its momentary inconvenience, or with false pride, many of us would rather let somebody else do it, if indeed we think about it at all: "Who wants to pick up beer cans, anyway?" Such a supercilious attitude is an ingredient of community suicide and is as bad, regardless of our socioeconomic status, as those who toss beer cans, Coke cups, or fast food sacks out of car windows.

At other times we were impressed to refer on these pages to practices which normally are not discussed in "polite" company. But we, along with some of you, think they had better be written if we are to survive—including such fixtures as the common flush toilet—lest we be forced one day to resort to practices of primitive countries as India or return to great-grandad's back yard installations.

## Some Things to Remember

There are several items which may slip by you as you read this book, but if you remember them, your reading may be greatly enriched. For many years in the administration of schools, colleges, and universities, I have found it wise to clearly define such power lines as philosophy, goals, resources, and methods. We believe these are as important considerations in families as in institutions, so we mention them here and again in closing this book.

- Philosophy. We hope that your philosophy will see money as only one objective in establishing a family industry, but that preparing your children in ethics and leadership will be even more important; such motives will likely bring even greater profit.

- Goals. Share the development of your goals with your spouse and children and others who may be involved.

- Resources. Seek sound counsel and all other resources possible.

- Methods. Plan carefully so that you use the most simple, efficient, and honest materials and methods you can find. Then work your plan. Look down the road; think, for instance, how you will make a transition when a child leaves home either temporarily or for long term.

Your goals are understated if you don't think of building integrity, dependability, order, cleanliness, and similar qualities in your children and other employees, if any. You should have in mind a growth program for each. For example, are you making your oldest child the company president? If not, why not? How about the other children or employees? Are you taking special note of each individual's assets and capitalizing on them? You can make clear to all that each has unique talents, and it's good management to use them.

Have you made an effort to learn from others who are in the same type of business as you? Where have been their unique successes or failures? Will you profit by these? We have provided many stories of successful home businesses with this very factor in mind.

It is crucial to embrace sound business ethics and principles, remembering that these are universal and apply to home industries as well as out-of-home businesses. They are our basic reasons for actions. For example, be sure that:

- You are communicating accurately and fully, even within your family, and that any communication breakdowns are cleared up to the satisfaction of all concerned.

- All involved understand that authority can only be granted when each accepts commensurate responsibility.

- All understand that any problems with honesty, accuracy, or conflict among "employees" can ruin an otherwise strong business potential. And violations of your (and their) established principles or practices must have their penalties. You may eventually also want to set down an arbitration or conciliation method when children become old enough to handle it.

Most of our stories apply only to a specific business or trade, but a number are diversified, to encourage families to meet the various interests and motives of their children and to give some idea of the astonishing variety possible in a home—depending on location, differences in seasons, size of family, and many other considerations.

Sometimes we use several stories to emphasize or broaden a particularly important thought, as when we discuss values, manners, and thoughtfulness. When appropriate and available, we have included names and places. In yet others we have adapted stories deliberately to avoid identification or for some other reason, but in each instance the essential details are accurate and the story true. Our aim here is for integrity, salted here and there with a little humor and a lot of practical common sense.

Occasionally we repeat a facet of management or reference in another chapter. If so, it's to emphasize a point which might be easy to overlook or to continue a theme which is designed to run like a golden thread through the book, like the idea of sacrificing present pleasures for future benefits—which is highly appropriate to all chapters here.

We are acutely aware of our common emphases on the closeness of parents and other adults with children, and the possibility that our readers might think we are totally consumed with home education. While we are certain, given a reasonably sound home environment, that children should be much more with their parents especially in their early years, we have set out here to provide principles and methods which apply to all families.

We also make reference to other books we have written which fill out certain chapters here such as health, discipline, or the most enjoyable, effective, and inexpensive home education. All of them are carefully documented. We welcome any questions or challenges on points we have tried to effectively mak

# PART ONE

# HOW TO MANAGE
# YOUR HOME

# ONE MAN'S FAMILY

I was a member of one man's family who learned about home management with unnecessary pain. We were poignant examples of what *not* to do. I learned lessons which may have you saying, "Just like me" or "But for the grace of God, there go I." My dad was a wonderful father, a hard worker, and money earner who taught his children how to work. This was a great gift with possible eternal consequences. He was a man of unusual principle and offered such high quality in his business that he never had to advertise. I know of only one place he fell short: He could not save from what he earned.

### The C. D. Moores

Dad had lost our mother in the "flu" epidemic of 1918–19 at the end of World War I and stayed single for five years before he married my second-grade teacher. Although she was an excellent teacher, she was as short on economy skills as Dad. The idea of sacrificing present pleasures for future benefits would have been about as popular at our home as a New Age preacher in an old-fashioned revival meeting.

## Following the Dream

Dad was a prosperous building contractor whose work few could match in southern California. A wide array of clients pursued him—developers, movie stars, paving contractors, institutions. And he spent as if the future would always be secure. We had new cars every year, sometimes more often, and always with "good reasons." We went to the best private schools, and we always had all we needed to eat and to wear. Always thoughtful of his kids, Dad bought a fine dairy ranch at Selma in the San Joaquin Valley of central California to give them an experience "out of the city." His usual success soon called for more pasture, so he bought another near Kingsburg. And yet another beckoned—a luxuriant grape and alfalfa farm out of nearby Caruthers that was "too good to miss."

Property poor, you say? No, not exactly; but yes, almost! Dad was sometimes earning over five hundred dollars a day from his various jobs in an era when ten dollars daily was top pay for skilled labor. If all had gone as he had planned, the ranches and farms would have been paid up in two or three years. Or if we had not been spending beyond our needs on new cars, a fine piano, organ, vibra-harp, on building and maintaining a swimming pool, and on and on.

Dad's dream was expanding, and soon his two oldest boys were out on the farm, learning in summers what it means to roll out of bed at four in the morning to massage the milk from a herd of Jersey and Guernsey cows—the best, of course—and to tend the births of their calves. Then we would shovel manure until breakfast, go to the field where in midday we mowed and raked alfalfa behind a choice pair of mules, and after a few days drying time, loaded the hay on a wagon pulled by the same critters. I'll never forget the irritation of dry alfalfa leaves on our sweaty backs as we pitch-forked the hay overhead.

I was the younger of the two, and the stronger, a full twelve years old in the middle of 1928. And much was expected, for Dad wanted his boys to be "rightly-trained." I didn't think much of Dad's dream in those days, but we bragged in our small talk with nearby farmers, and with relatives and friends back home in southern California. We were receiving eighty-five cents a pound for butterfat—a payment measure for milk—the highest in the state. And our butterfat content was very high, as should be expected of a fine Jersey/Guernsey herd. Why shouldn't Dad buy more farms? Any good businessman must assess such risks. And why shouldn't these dreams come true?

## The Crash of 1929

But my father didn't fully assess those risks. He was not aware of the goings-on in the New York Stock Market and its heady "bull" market. The only bull we knew was that great big Jersey that faithfully serviced our cows and gave us some of the best calves in the county. Then one otherwise beautiful autumn morning in 1929, we read in big black headlines that the Stock Market had crashed. This had little meaning to us, for we didn't own any stocks. But we soon learned that when that kind of catastrophe hits, everyone suffers.

Dad came up from southern California to see us every week or so to "check on things" and to assuage our perennial homesickness. On one of these evenings after work, he opened his mail and fell into a rare, deep silence.

"Bad news?" we asked fearfully.

"The price of butterfat," he groaned. "It's dropped from eighty-five to twenty-six cents overnight."

Our three farms went down like dominoes. The Kingsburg place which provided pasture for the Selma dairy farm went first. Then the beautiful grape and alfalfa place at Caruthers. And finally the dairy itself, and all those beautiful Jerseys and Guernseys, even their manure, whose value I had come to know. Somehow Dad managed to hold on to our heavily-mortgaged home in Montrose, but the bank took a lot of his heavy equipment and our new, best car. The equipment loss could have been more serious, except that with the massive depression that ensued, there wasn't much work to do, and when Dad did land jobs, the pay was less than before.

But we all knuckled under. Dad had the kind of spirit that makes great men, great fathers. He was a man of muscle and faith.

And our stepmother backed him well. Dad and Mother and we six youngsters lived mostly on potatoes, beans, and "day-old" bread which more likely had aged a week. We scrimped on electricity and gas and put bricks in the flush tank to save water. With no money for gasoline, we walked the two miles to and from school.

For Dad, the most humiliating experience of all was forced bankruptcy. But Dad promised all his creditors that one day, if he lived, he would pay back every cent. He did live, and none of us can forget when he came home to announce proudly and gratefully that every debt was paid. We went out for ice cream cones that night.

It seemed we had been victims of events beyond our control. Why should we suffer for stock market sins? We could also ask why anyone should suffer from hurricane, tornado, earthquake, fire, or flood. I did a lot of thinking when I went away to college at sixteen with twenty-five dollars in my pocket, to work my way through college by mixing concrete and milking cows, this time at *two* in the morning. There might just be some wisdom in putting aside enough for a "rainy day" and avoid overextending oneself in any kind of credit. People who were not in debt did not suffer the losses we did.

We were just "getting on our feet" when disaster struck again. A cloudburst capped several days of heavy rain in Montrose and Glendale, California; the weather man later said that we had eighteen inches of rain in a little more than half an hour. We lived in the foothills where no one ever thought of a flood, but the combination of forest fires the year before, the soaked ground just before the downpour, and the cloudburst itself brought a flood of water down from the mountains that hit our home at roof height, and left mud up to our piano keys. Fortunately all of our family were saved when we ran to our back porch. All the houses across the street, much larger than ours, were swept away.

So it was back to diluted milk, used clothes, and the general plight of the homeless. I dropped out of college for two years to drive a truck, wheel concrete, fix a brown-bag lunch of wheat bread and peanut butter, and help Dad build once again.

Still we did not learn. Dad rebuilt on the same lot, but his idea, instead of saving, was to defy future floods: We built a solid concrete house. It had such appeal that he shortly sold it at a good profit, and we built another house nearby. There he installed a fine badminton court, a better swimming pool, and new furniture.

## College and on My Own

Eventually I went back to college, to work virtually my entire way, for there were no government aid programs in those days and few if any small college grants. My scholarship was a back-strengthening job firing boilers with four-foot logs, and serving an apprenticeship as a "plumber's friend." I managed a twenty-five cent haircut every six to eight weeks and meticulously cared for my one cheap blue-gray suit which someone had thoughtfully given me: no cleaning bills, no unnecessary wear. I seldom left the campus, not because of discipline, but for the few cents it took to travel.

And I learned more than science and humanities. I learned something about why and how to set priorities—to find what was really of first importance, and accept it despite my natural appetites or inclinations to the contrary. And I learned a bit about the healing balm of humor, not clowning, mind you, nor idle talk, but studying—and sometimes struggling—to make a happy exchange instead of a harsh one. I believe that this helped us over many a rugged hurdle in administering schools, colleges, and universities, not to mention family life.

One of our professors, Dr. Guy Wolfkill, had a formula for setting priorities that has guided us for the rest of our lives. His only obvious problem was trying to hide the stub of his left arm after he lost his left hand in an accident. Yet working with only one hand didn't seem to make much difference to him. He got more manual work done in his spare time than anybody on our Napa Valley, California, campus; he turned his home site into a beautifully-landscaped garden.

But we were certain that there must be something beyond his prodigious manual labors. And there was. It came out in class one day when he gave us in one short sentence a lesson we have never forgotten: *"If you want to succeed at the highest level, you must learn to manage your life by sacrificing present pleasures for future benefits."* This, we subsequently found, can and must be applied to every appetite and phase in life: to what we eat, drink, or whatever we do, even to the extent of worrying too much about having every speck of dust wiped from our coffee tables or the floors—and silver—weekly polished. These may give us pleasure, but there may be personal and family needs which far outweigh these momentarily satisfying preferences.

When I finished college in 1938, I had few dollars in my pocket, but no debts! I didn't have all A's as I had hoped; in fact I had only about a B or B-plus average and enjoyed no academic honors. Yet I had so many good experiences and the prospect of more—including marriage to one of the world's great women— that my shortage of superior scholarship was neither necessary nor surprising, given an ordinary mind and a forty- to fifty-hour work week while in college—extending to eighty hours during vacations.

I was comforted with another gem from a favorite Wolfkill author: "An ordinary mind, well disciplined, will accomplish more and higher things than the most highly-educated mind and greatest talents without self-control." Hard work and self-discipline were teaching me lessons that one day would guide colleges and universities out of debt.

## The Nels Nelsons

Dorothy Nelson was waiting for me, already out of college and on her teaching job. Dorothy, too, had learned the hard way. Our marriage united two families who had been hard hit by financial losses. Her parents had been prosperous South Dakotans who chose around the end of World War I to sell their large farm and head for California. A combination of disappointments in the early 1920s, typical of investing for investment's sake and city slickers taking advantage of naive ex-farmers, made the wealthy Nels Nelsons as poor as the once-wealthy C. D. Moores.

## Self-Sufficient Farmers

Yet a remnant of their "fortune" remained. They still had four al-kali acres clear of debt in the little dairy town of Artesia which gave them a place to start again. The family of six, two sons and two daughters, set up housekeeping in a tent while "Pop" built a house the size of a double garage. Since at the time it was a dairy community, he added a dairy next door which he rented out, and also a service station which he ran in their front yard. Their thrifty Norwegian background stood them in good stead as Mom and the four children grew a garden and raised chickens and turkeys in the back yard. Home-baked bread, milk from the nearby dairy, and produce from their back yard allowed them to live, they thought, like kings. Because Mom was an excellent seamstress, the children went to school in new dresses and shirts made from remnants and didn't know they were poor.

By the time the Great Depression hit, Dorothy's folks were self-sufficient enough not to be jarred very much. In fact, after things settled down a bit, Pop bought several lots downtown in Artesia for fifty dollars each—forfeited by those who could not pay their taxes during the depression—and built houses to sell or rent. During her first year of teaching, Dorothy bought three of these lots, one of which we used to build our first house.

## Our Experience

Dorothy had experienced enough of both prosperity and loss to understand the value of money management and has since done a great job of helping me to grasp lessons my parents never did learn. We decided, mostly at Dorothy's initiative, to live on one salary so that we could be well on our way to completing our education and owning our home before starting our family. That settled another matter which often intrudes in home management: Who will control the family purse? I asked Dorothy to be the family treasurer.

I had enough responsibility through the years, as elementary school teacher in California's Hermosa Beach, U. S. Army staff officer and commander in San Francisco, New Guinea, and Manila, city school superintendent in Artesia, teaching fellow at the University of Southern California, college dean and president, university vice-president, U.S. Office of Education officer, head of an advanced study center out of Southern Illinois University and the University of Chicago, and finally, directing not-for-profit research foundations. Those successful institutional management years were based on the simple home management principles which I learned with Dorothy's coaching through years of successful personal finance.

## Budgeting

For at least two decades we listed every penny spent. Not only dollars, mind you, but *pennies,* too—a practice we strongly recommend to everybody who needs to establish some frugality cells in his blood. It used to be said that a penny saved is a penny earned, but that was before income, sales, and a number of other hidden taxes. Now a penny saved is worth considerably more than a penny earned.

We budgeted for rent, food, clothes, and tithes, and lived within our budget. We bought clothes or anything "pre-owned" that we *needed* and which was of real quality. Bargains, no matter how cheap, are not bargains if they do not fill a real need. We saved electricity with sailor showers, cut transportation down to bare bones, did very little eating out, bought little or no chewing gum, soft drinks, ice cream cones, nor entertainment. We lived on half the budget of most of our newly-married friends.

Does this sound austere, boring, or overly ascetic? Actually, it became a fun game. We did have a special night out after teaching once a week when we did our shopping at the Grand Central (wholesale) Market in Los Angeles, ate out at Schrader's Cafeteria with its delicious low-cost food and live dinner music in those days, and then went to our graduate class at USC. When we came home afterward, we zwiebacked (twice-baked) most of the day-old bread in the oven and crowded the rest of it in the refrigerator with the produce we had purchased. Milk came from a wholesale dairy outlet and only occasionally did we need to go to a regular grocery store to stock up on staples.

We sensed no deprivation for we kept busy on the job during the school year and in graduate classes at the university. We had an exciting life just getting started, making new friends, doing church and community work, leading a Boy Scout troop, and building and furnishing our first home. And in all of this we learned some more lessons in the economics of borrowing, buying, and selling.

## Ownership

We bought our first used refrigerator by paying half down and the rest in thirty days. We bought a new Ford on a six-month contract. We took out a FHA loan to build our first home, sold it for thirty-five hundred dollars when we had to move to Hermosa Beach, and never borrowed again. Not that we wouldn't borrow if we had to, but we determined to live within our means even if the Joneses had other ideas; we avoided debt like the plague.

In one of our most important early economics lessons, the buyer of our first home wanted to relocate and was in a hurry to sell. He apologetically asked if we would like to buy it back for the same price as we had sold it. By that time I was on U. S. Army active duty in New Guinea. Nevertheless, we gladly bought it back, not because we were sophisticated about housing markets, but because we knew the house was a good one, well located, and would provide a home for Dorothy who went back to teaching in my absence. We realized a year later what a good buy we had made when we were offered sixty-five hundred dollars. So we sold it to the delight of Dorothy's folks who wanted her to live with them, worried that it might not be safe for her to live alone.

Today that house would sell for over sixty-five thousand dollars. We learned about quality, economy, and location which stood us in good stead as over many years we built seven more houses in places where we were assigned to work and all sold profitably.

We will talk more in a later chapter about profitably locating, building, and buying. Yet we underscore the principles of early frugality and avoiding carelessness in little things can keep you from the pain of financial disaster in big things. And we add that the big thing is often disheartened children or worse, a broken marriage. The lessons here are for parents, but also by precept and example, for children. Poor financial management can threaten a home and sometimes break it up completely, for financial distress is one of marriage's, and family's, starkest enemies. But the security and self-discipline of a well-managed family is a proven path to domestic happiness and peace.

# TWO

# HOW TO COACH YOUNG FINANCIERS

O ne day while waiting to do another broadcast with Dr. James Dobson, we were talking about home management when he mentioned an interview he was planning with a Southerner by the name of Larry Burkett. That tickled our curiosity, but the real excitement didn't come until sometime later when we were broadcasting with Al Sanders in California, and he introduced us to Larry. Then we began to get an idea of the completeness of his program—which reflected the very ideals we had been pursuing in our home for over fifty years.

There would be few families suffering privation or struggling with debt if they carefully followed Larry's counsel. He has thought through systematically a number of principles and practices that should be in any good home management book, so we are, with his permission, adapting in this chapter several segments of his new book, *The Complete Financial Guide for Young Couples*— just enough, we believe, to excite your appetite for the rich fare he has to offer.[1]

We had not read Larry's new book until we had nearly completed the manuscript for the book you are reading. We were happily surprised at the way the two manuscripts meshed in both principle and practice. What he is preaching, we have been largely practicing for fifty-two years at this writing. Although you will not hear him speaking in the same words, you will repeatedly sense the threads that run through our books; for instance, about planning, and granting authority to your children but requiring commensurate responsibility. An example is his discussion about operating and buying cars and "renting" rooms to your own children. And you will discern the principle of sacrificing present pleasures for future benefits.

Here is his message, with occasional bracketed comments from us. He writes first of training children about ages one to ten, then ages eleven to sixteen, and finally seventeen to twenty. *

≈ ≈ ≈

## Training Children Ages One to Ten

Normally during the first ten years, the basic attitudes of your children are being formed. [You understand, of course that children vary in maturity, as Larry later emphasizes, and the ages given in this chapter may vary considerably, depending on the child's rate of development.] You're not going to change their basic personalities no matter what you do. But you can mold their character by reinforcing their strong points and correcting their flaws. The way they manage money is merely a measure of their strengths and weaknesses.

For young children, you need to assign some nonpaying jobs, such as cleaning their rooms, doing the dishes, and picking up their toys. All children need some basic responsibilities for which they don't get paid. My children used to object because I started implementing this philosophy in our family, admittedly a bit late. They usually felt like they should get paid for everything they did.

---

* The rest of the chapter is adapted from *The Complete Financial Guide for Young Couples* by Larry Burkett. (Wheaton, IL: Victor Books, 1989). Used by permission.

The point I tried to get across was, we're all part of a society and each of us has things we *have* to do. I would usually point out that if I didn't get paid for changing their diapers when they were young, they don't get paid for taking out the garbage now.

You should also provide some paying jobs for your children [and/or get them involved in a cottage industry as suggested throughout this book]. These might include lawn care, cleaning the garage, washing the car, and so on. There are a variety of things for which you should pay your children, and you should pay them equitably, according to what you are able to afford [and we might add, according to their maturity and the quality of their performance].

When we lived in Tucker, Georgia (just outside Atlanta), we owned a house on a steep hill; in fact, if you stepped onto my front yard without baseball cleats on, you could end up in my back yard! So obviously, it was a tough lawn to mow. My oldest son was very compliant; whatever I asked him to do, he did it. When I said, "Please mow the lawn," he mowed it, and whatever I paid him was okay, within reason.

My second son questioned everything (If you ever have a child who says, "Why?" then you'll understand.) He had ninety-nine ways to use the word *why*. When he turned twelve, he became eligible to mow our lawn.

The first thing he asked was, "How much?" I said, "I'll pay you seven dollars."

He replied, "It's not worth it. I'm not going to mow that lawn for seven dollars.

I said, "That's okay, but that's the only way you have to earn money. If you don't do it, you don't get any money, you understand that."

He said, "Sure Dad. But I'm not going to mow that lawn for seven dollars."

So I went to a friend who had a son about the same age, and negotiated with him to mow the lawn for seven dollars. He was there within five minutes, mowing my lawn. Every week after that my son mowed our lawn. He decided, if it was worth it to his friend, it was worth it to him.

You need to be fair with your children but also firm. There are some simple rules to observe. I believe that's true with our children as well. If you want to train your children to be good employees, you must take on the role of an employer. Therefore, you have to establish some principles that any reasonable employer would.

## Pay Them Only for Jobs That Are Completed

I told my children from the beginning, you don't get 90 percent of the money for 90 percent of the job. You get 100 percent of the money for 100 percent of the job. In other words, if you don't finish, you don't get paid. Why? Because no employer is going to pay for a partially finished job. What if an employee decided, "I don't want to work five days a week, so I'll only work four days?" Do you think an employer would agree? Hardly so; most employers expect a full week's work. It would be like a car painter saying, "I don't like painting a whole car. I'll just paint half of it, so just pay me for the half I paint." It just doesn't work that way.

## Pay for Quality Work

I tried to share with my children that they need to be the best that they can be. That doesn't mean that they can be the best in the world; they may not have that ability. It means that they should be the best they are capable of being. If employees would only follow the Golden Rule, there would be few unemployed. First, give honor to the authority over them, doing everything possible to promote that authority. Second, do the best job possible within their abilities.

## Pay Fairly, Within Your Budget, But Don't Overpay Because You Can Afford It

I have a good friend who has lived to regret this practice. When his children went to work for him, he started them out at about eight dollars an hour. By the time they graduated from high school, they were making nearly twenty dollars an hour! When they went to college, he bought each of them a brand new automobile. Then when they graduated from college he decided they were on their own and no longer his "responsibility." Unfortunately, he had preconditioned their expectations. They had made twenty dollars an hour mowing lawns and drove new cars in college. What employer would be able to match that? None, they found out. His children still shift from job to job, looking for that executive position that will match their expectations.

You need to be very careful that you don't overpay. Remember the principles that you're trying to build into your children's lives have to sustain them throughout their lifetimes. So pay fairly, but don't overpay.

## Use Visual Reinforcement, Especially For Young Children

Most parents find that a chart on the back of a door works very well. Not every child is motivated by charts, but most are. My number-two son could have cared less about charts. He would say, "Forget the stars. How much does it pay?" Not literally, but almost that bad.

Most young children are motivated by praise and rewards, and charts serve that function well. One thing children will demand is honesty. If you say a star represents a job well done, be sure you're faithful to that rule. Almost always one child, especially a girl, will be the guardian of the rules. Children will be sure to let you know if you're not true to your word, and well they should. If you don't really mean it, don't say it.

## Teach Your Children "Sharing" Principles

One thing I encourage you to avoid is the "quarter-in-the-plate" syndrome. Many parents fall into that trap. There they are in church, the offering plate is coming around, so they give their children a quarter to drop in. That means absolutely nothing to most of them. They didn't earn the money, it didn't cost them anything, and so giving becomes a religious ritual. I would encourage you to avoid that. It's best for your children to give only if it costs them something.

Help your children get involved with the needs of people. With most children what works best is to have them invest directly in the lives of other people, particularly the poor. Once they see that giving as a golden rule is sharing a surplus where others have a lack, it will become real to them. I know children who have supported orphans for several years, and they still get letters from those they were helping. Now they're grown and many have their own families. This helps children understand the purpose as well as the principle of giving. It isn't just dropping money in a plate. It's being involved in the lives of other people. Once a child is committed to that concept, nobody has to force him to give.

If you must force your children to give, somewhere along the way they'll get big enough to stop. If they give because of principle, nobody will ever talk them out of it. I have met four- and five-year-old children who were committed to giving funds they had earned and felt it a privilege to do so. Some were able to give only a dime or a quarter, but they gave to meet the needs of another. A quarter isn't much in America, but in Mexico it will buy a day's food.

## Teach Your Children to Save

It's hard to understand why so many parents who have had bitter experiences with debt, including divorce, fail to teach their children how to avoid it. In reality, any parent can discourage debt simply by encouraging saving. After all, we need "things" (kids do too) and must either save or borrow to get them.

While teaching a group of seminary students on the Biblical principles of managing money, I found myself counseling virtually every free minute. These were students about to graduate into careers as pastors and missionaries who were deep in debt. Most had student loans that stretched back seven and eight years. Others had credit card debts, car loans, bank loans, and family loans. Without realizing it, most of these potential leaders had doomed their careers and marriages through excessive borrowing. Few churches would be able to pay salaries sufficient to meet their needs, and virtually no mission groups could.

A young man named Jeremy shared that his father had started him saving at a very early age and promised to match his saving dollar-for-dollar if he wouldn't touch it for ten years. He worked the normal kid's jobs: a paper route, summer work, washing cars, etc. He had used some of his savings to purchase a pressure cleaner for sidewalks while in high school and started going door-to-door, cleaning driveways and sidewalks. After that, he was self-employed.

By the time he started college, he owned a car and had over twenty thousand dollars in savings. He supplemented his savings by working at his business during vacations and summers. His father paid for one half of his college expenses, and he paid the other half.

When he graduated from college and entered seminary, he sold his cleaning business for twenty-five thousand dollars and used five thousand dollars to purchase a parking lot striping machine. So he entered seminary debt-free and with twenty thousand dollars in savings. He again supplemented his savings by painting stripes on small parking lots. That business grew to where he employed four other students. He was about to graduate from seminary and had sold his latest business for forty thousand dollars. The only difference between Jeremy and the vast majority of other students was that his father started him on sound principles of handling money at an early age. Solomon wisely said, "Train up a child in the way he should go: and when he is old, he will not depart from it" (Proverbs 22:6, KJV).

## Training Children Ages Eleven to Sixteen

At ages eleven to sixteen, you need to increase your children's level of understanding about finances. There are a few basic principles that parents need to concentrate on during this transition period to adulthood.

## There Should Be No Such Thing as an Allowance

An allowance implies money given by a parent but disassociated from performance. Look around and you'll see the products of "allowing" parents at any university in America today. What you really need to teach your teenagers is responsibility. They must understand that they must work if they want to eat. Obviously, you don't want to withhold food from a sixteen-year-old. But when it comes to your car, yes.

So many times parents indulge because they love, when indulgence is the exact opposite of real love; *real* love does what is best for the other person, regardless of the difficulties for you.

It's an interesting phenomenon that children grow up resenting a parent who was too harsh, but they also resent a parent who was too lenient. I have heard many mothers say they don't understand why their children resent them later in life when all they ever did was give, give, give. That is *exactly* the problem. They buffered their children rather than trained them.

## Have a Very Strict Performance Code
## For Work Your Teenagers Do

In our seminar on principles for operating a business, we teach what happens when employers don't establish definitive standards for employees. The employees don't know what is expected.

We need to establish standards for our children, including timeliness, dependability, attitude, and honor. These are the standards by which God evaluates success or failure.

I have a friend who uses his business to provide job opportunities for young people just starting out. He says he is continually amazed at the lack of responsibility on the part of many young people, even from Christian homes. He expects no special knowledge from the teenagers he hires, but he has two absolute standards: be to work on time every day and maintain a good attitude.

If they adhere to these standards and *try*, he will train them thoroughly. He told me the story of Greg, a young man he hired. Greg came from a broken home and had been raised by a Christian grandmother. When Greg came to his company through a work-study program at his high school, he was enthusiastic about a chance to work at something with a future.

Greg proved to be bright and enthusiastic but on the undisciplined side. He was prompt and dependable for the first couple of weeks, but he then began to be late periodically and call in with a variety of excuses for why he couldn't come to work.

My friend suffered through Greg's bad habits until summer because Greg showed such promise when he *was* working. After being disciplined, he would improve for awhile and then lapse back into his bad habits.

During the summer school break, Greg was employed full-time. But he was often tardy and periodically just didn't show up at all. Each time he was apologetic, but the cycle continued. In conversations with his grandmother, she said, "He loves his job, but that boy just can't get out of bed in the mornings." She asked the owner to please not fire Greg. "He wants to work; he just never had a real job before."

Finally, in desperation, my friend sent one of his supervisors by Greg's home in the mornings to get him up and in to work. As normal Greg was ready for the first few days, but then lapsed into sleeping late. The supervisor told Greg's grandmother, "You put a full pitcher of water in the refrigerator every night. I'll get him up."

The next day when he came, Greg was still asleep. He took the pitcher of *very* cold water and went into Greg's room. He said, "Greg, you going to work today?"

"Yes, sir," Greg replied, "in a minute," and he went back to sleep.

His sleep was interrupted by two quarts of nearly-freezing water.

He fussed and fumed while he was getting dried off and dressed for work. His grandmother cackled, "I'll leave that mess for you to clean up tonight!"

The next day the whole routine repeated itself. The third day when the supervisor came to get Greg, he asked his grandmother if he was still in bed. She said, "Well, he got up, but I believe he's asleep again." When she opened the refrigerator door to get the pitcher, Greg heard it and leapt out of the bed, fully clothed!

As time passed, Greg became one of the most valued employees this company had. He is now a plant manager with children of his own. You can be certain that he is teaching his children to do their work well, on time, and with dependability. Greg often says to his sons, "If a stranger loved me enough to hold me accountable for my work habits, I sure can do as much for you boys."

Remember that the earlier you start instilling the right habits in your children, the easier it is. It's *never* too late, but the earlier, the better.

## Reward Extra Effort

If your children are excellent at what they do and put forth extra effort, they should be rewarded for doing a superior job.

It's important that your children understand the no work, no pay principle. But it is just as important that they understand the better-work, better-pay principle.

You can begin to teach this principle even at the youngest ages by acknowledging when a child puts out extra effort. That does not mean equal performance necessarily. Each child has differing abilities and what may be extra effort to one may be coasting to another. You need to be able to evaluate when a child is trying harder. One of our sons tended to be a perfectionist, even as a small child. Picking up his clothes and toys and cleaning his room were natural for him. As a result, he was praised and rewarded. Any parent who wouldn't do so would be a little crazy. Another son tended to be messy and rarely, if ever, noticed his disorder. When he took the time and effort to pick up his things or clean his room, he was looking for praise (or money). The more often we did so, the more normal it became for him. From time to time we raised our standards for rewards. It probably took three years before his norm reached the other son's low average. But had we never rewarded him in the beginning, the process would never have started. It is effort, not skill level, you must measure and commend.

## Stick to Your Convictions

Don't be swayed into lowering your standards simply because you have Christian friends who do. Sometimes the most conflicting value system you'll find is in a Christian school. When your children are in contact with other children from Christian homes and find their values are not the same, they will challenge your rules.

Unfortunately, many Christian parents don't pay by any performance standards and buy their children virtually anything they want, anytime they want it. The sad thing is that they actually believe this demonstrates love. The tendency is to be swayed in doing the same thing for your children. Don't compound their error. Remember Solomon again: "He that spareth his rod hateth his son; but he that loveth him chasteneth him betimes" (Proverbs 13:24, KJV).

Discipline is not for punishment. It is to set boundaries for your children. Within those boundaries they are secure. One of the major difficulties children have today is that they are being asked to make adult decisions before they're ready. The world makes an almost unbelievable array of temptations available to them at a very young age. Parents should be their buffers. Set your standards and stick to them. Many times I will volunteer to teach classes at various Christian schools [as well as others] just to get a feel for where Christian families are in the training of their children. I have to be honest and say it's rather depressing, with few exceptions.

I like to take surveys of how these kids have been trained. I usually ask questions such as: How many are assigned chores that take an hour a week or more? (about 10 percent) How many have to earn their allowances? (about 10 percent) How many receive allowances of five dollars a week or more (about 50 percent) How many believe their parents should control how they spend their money? (about 2 percent) How many have parents that require a budget? (about 2 percent) How many believe their parents handle their money well, based on family arguments? (about 10 percent) How many would like to be like their parents? (about 10 percent)

This is by no means a scientific survey, but it does demonstrate that parents are neglecting a fundamental area of education for their children. If you don't set your own standards and stick to them, your children will be the losers.

## Teach Teenagers the Principle of Budgeting

Like Dad and Mom, teenagers also should know well the condition of their "herds and flocks." In other words, they should know where their money goes before they spend it.

It is important to me for my children to get my counsel before they get married. A mistake in choosing the right partner can result in grief for a lot of people, me included. My oldest son came and shared that he wanted to get married. After getting to know his fiancée, I said, "I approve of your choice; she is a great girl. But before you get married, I want to see a budget that shows what you will earn and how you plan to spend it for the first year." I never doubted his ability to budget in his own family because he budgeted his money well when he lived at home. It was a sparse but workable budget, and they made it.

It's sad to see how many young couples don't make it because they get married with no financial training at all. If you think the schools will do this training for you, think again. For years I tried to get Christian schools to establish a basic home finance class and make it mandatory for graduation. Even after writing the curriculum for it, I found virtually no takers.

Since it wasn't a part of the "approved" curriculum by accreditation groups, they couldn't spare the time. I wondered whatever happened to God's accreditation system. I have since taken the material into homes and churches where it has been enthusiastically adopted. I'll share a few of the ideas in the next [section].

Don't expect your children to jump up and down with joy when you begin to enforce financial discipline, including a budget. I remember when my strong-willed son (hardheaded) was about twelve years old and I started him on a budget. He had been used to spending his money, which he earned, pretty much the way he desired. I knew a budget was in his best interest, but he didn't see it that way at all.

We were about three weeks into the budgeting process, which included about half of his money going into savings, when he came into my office one day and said, "Dad, this is not a very democratic way to run a family." I said, "You're right, Son, and don't forget you don't live in a democracy in our home: You live in a benevolent dictatorship."

He mumbled and grumbled from time to time because he couldn't stand to think about unspent money. But he survived and we did too.

Later he joined the Marine reserves, where he went through boot camp training and then through a year of electronics training. I was speaking in California, where he was stationed, and I decided to drive out to see him one Sunday afternoon.

You need to realize that the whole time my son was living at home, he was always arguing, "Dad, this isn't right, that isn't right, I don't agree with that." Whatever rule I established, he wanted to stretch it. He would stretch it until he reached my boundaries, and then he would back off.

But that day in California, he said something that made all the grief we had endured worthwhile. He said, "Dad, I never told you how much I appreciate what you've done for me. You established discipline in my life that I don't see in most of the other guys I'm around. They cry and they complain and then they wash out because they've never learned to discipline themselves." It was worth all the years of struggling to see the end results in his life. It was worse on me than it was on him, though he probably would not agree with that at all.

As I said earlier, a general guide in budgeting for your children is very simple. The first part of their income should go to God.

The question is often asked, "Should I force my children to tithe?" I personally would not. At ages one to ten, I would encourage them and tell them to do it, because you're developing the principles in their lives. At eleven to sixteen, it should be their choice, because you need to find out whether they "believe" what you've been teaching them.

About 25 percent of their earnings should be put into a savings account for short-term use. The next 25 percent should be saved for long-term needs, and about 40 percent should be theirs to spend according to an approved budget.

By the way, I encourage parents not to just drop these principles on their kids. The first step is to put them into your own life and then start sharing them with your children.

I had a young woman call me one time after a seminar. She said, "You have ruined my life."

"How have I ruined your life?" I asked. At that seminar I had been talking about paying for college education, and I shared with the group what we do with our children. We pay half and they pay half.

She said, "You've ruined my life. I came home on spring break from college, and my dad said, 'You can't go back until you earn half of your tuition.'"

I said, "You tell him, he's absolutely wrong. Number one, I didn't tell him that was a Biblical principle. I said it was what *we* did. Second, he can't drop that on you during spring break." You must start such a plan at least ten years before the first child enters college. You can't just decide to implement it on an impulse. Don't provoke your children to anger.

Try to make your children a part of the planning process in your home, not the object of it. Share your budget with your children, just the same way they must share theirs with you.

## Training Children Ages Seventeen to Twenty

Some of you reading this book probably don't have teenagers yet, much less young adults. In fact, some of you probably fit into this age group yourselves. That's all right, we have all been seventeen to twenty at one time or another, and all of our children will be. This is a crucial age, because these are the transition years to adulthood.

By this time the basics of personal finances must be understood and applied or the mistakes of past generations will be repeated. Here I would like to discuss the essentials that children should be taught while under their parents' authority.

## Work/Vocation

The essential step is to determine the personality, skills, and gifts that God has given to each of your children. In our generation, it is not abnormal for young men and women to graduate from college and have no idea what they want to do vocationally. All too often they take any job that is available, only to find out later that they dislike the career field. Usually it's because personality and career field are mismatched.

Marsha was an example of this mismatch between personality and vocation. She had studied accounting in college and graduated with good grades. She took a job with an auditing company and found that she dreaded the daily routine. The only part of her job she enjoyed was when she could work on problem solving.

Her father, an accountant for a big-eight firm, sent her to a vocational counselor who discovered the cause of her discomfort. She had a creative personality that required frequent change and challenging tasks. The last thing she needed was routine functions. He recommended that she go to a law school (a long-time desire) and study investigative law. She did so, and now she is an investigator with a government securities agency and loves it. Her father was wise enough to point her in the right direction.

The next step is to help your older teenagers gather some career facts. Even if you can't determine the exact career field before they get involved, usually you can help them avoid the ones where they wouldn't fit. Perhaps the simplest way is to talk to experienced and reliable people in those careers. Ask fundamental questions such as: *What kind of education is required? What training is required? What personality type performs best? What hours do you work?*

My daughter has always wanted to be a veterinarian, primarily because she loved animals. Later in college she changed her mind and decided that she wanted to be a physician. After many long conversations with friends of mine who are medical doctors, her career field changed to psychology. She found that she wasn't willing to pay the price (in time) that a physician pays. She was able to make that decision without wasting several years of schooling simply by talking with others who had already gone the route.

## Self-Determination

Within limits, from about sixteen or seventeen years on, you need to allow your children to make their own financial decisions. Certainly the decisions you allow will vary by age and personality, but the more opportunities you allow now, the clearer picture you'll have of what they will do later.

*Clothes.* As any mother of teenagers knows, it's hard to select the clothes that you can afford and they will wear. At some point you need to shift the decision-making process over to them.

I suggest a quarterly clothes budget be allocated and then allow teenagers to select their own wardrobes. Obviously, the parents need to establish some fundamental rules regarding modesty, price, and style. But the decision about where to shop and what to buy should be the teenagers'. There are some hazards in yielding this authority, but you need to bear in mind that as parents, you are raising future adults who will eventually have the sole right to make these decisions.

It's always enlightening to see earlier evaluations being revealed in your children's buying habits. It often helps parents to focus on weak areas, as well as strengths, in their children.

I recall the example of two teenagers whose parents decided to give them total responsibility for buying their clothes. They spent several hours discussing where to find the best buys, how to pick quality clothes, and so on. Then one fateful summer day, Mom dropped them off in the shopping mall with about two hundred dollars each to buy school clothes.

The oldest son, about sixteen and very conservative, bought exactly what they had discussed: tennis shoes, jeans, shirts, underwear, etc. The younger son, about thirteen and very strong-willed, bought a couple of pairs of socks, a silk-screened T-shirt, and a *very* expensive skateboard. Later that evening during their family time, his father said, "Rick, we gave you the right and responsibility to make your own decisions about what clothes to buy. Just remember, no more clothes money for at least three months."

Rick replied, "Don't you worry, Dad. I've got plenty of clothes for school."

Over the next couple of weeks Rick succeeded in virtually destroying his pants, shirts, and shoes practicing on his new skateboard. About three days before school was to start, Rick came downstairs where his dad was reading and said, "Dad, I have a problem. I can't go to school like this." He showed his tennis shoes with toes sticking out of them.

Rick's dad replied, "Oh, that's really a shame. You're right. You can't go to school like that." And with that, he got some black electrical tape and wrapped it around Rick's shoes. After three months of wearing ragged jeans and holey shoes, Rick got the idea that his parents were serious. His dad said his son still had some lessons to learn about money, but the next time he received his clothing budget, he bought what he needed.

*Cars.* Whether or not to allow your son or daughter to have a car in high school is a major decision, even if *they* buy it. But to provide them a car and cover all the expenses usually works to the long-term detriment of most teenagers. Obviously, there are exceptions but, in general, cars are a luxury and an indulgence for students. Too often they're given to keep the kids out of the parents' hair.

If you're going to allow your teenagers to use your vehicles, I would suggest some basic rules:

- They should pay for their own insurance.

- They should pay a portion of the maintenance and upkeep. I suggest a usage rate of five cents per mile.

- They should provide their own gas and oil.

- They should clean the car after every use or at least once per week.

- They should pay all of their traffic violations, and driving privileges should be suspended for serious violations.

Just the fact that a child pays for his or her own car expenses is not justification for giving them free rein. A car is a large expense and a distraction that costs many high school students their futures. Remember how much trouble cars are in your life and help your children avoid trouble. They may get irritated, but they'll get over it, I promise.

## Checking Accounts

Without hesitation, I can say that by age sixteen, your children should be using and maintaining their own checking accounts.

Since most teenagers can get along without checking accounts, most never have them. Even those that do often end up with a big mess where the parents pay for overdrafts and usually cancel the account. That is *not* an answer to poor management.

Remember that you're not raising children; you're raising future adults, and in our society checking accounts are a fact of life. Don't let your children leave home without the basic skills for survival. Teach your daughter to maintain and balance her checkbook properly, and one day your future son-in-law will call you blessed.

A small bribe in this area often helps motivate teenagers. In other words, promise them a financial reward for maintaining their checking accounts perfectly.

I would suggest a bonus of one hundred dollars (or whatever your budget can handle) for maintaining and balancing their checking accounts for a year. I would further encourage you to let them spend this money as they see fit (within reason) to give them additional incentive.

## Credit Cards

Contrary to popular opinion, I do recommend allowing children to use credit cards. Remember, credit cards are *not* the problem. It is the misuse of credit cards that creates the problems.

I personally believe it would be better if young couples didn't have access to so much credit. But in a society where the whole economy runs on debt, credit is a fact of life. So it's best to teach your children how to manage and control it, not vice versa.

I would suggest allowing them to have a credit card in their name at about age seventeen or eighteen. The rules for using the card should be clear, written, and absolute:

- The card can be used *only* for budgeted items—clothes, gas, tires, and so on.

- The account has to be paid in full each month—no exceptions.

- The *first* month the account isn't paid, take the card back and destroy it.

I have seen parents establish these rules and then fail to enforce them because of a sad tale of circumstances told by their teenager. To fail to keep the rules is to invite more violations. If you're not committed to enforcing the rules of credit, don't let your teenagers have a credit card. All you'll do is encourage debt. Debt is a great temptation that is virtually irresistible without stern control, as thousands of divorced young couples will attest. My record for teenage credit card debt was set by a young woman, about eighteen, when she went off to college at a state university.

Her father didn't want her to get caught without money should her car break down, so he arranged to have a credit card issued in her name. Unfortunately, she had no experience with such device and misused the card a little. In fact, she became the most popular girl on campus because she loaned her card out liberally.

At the end of her second month of college, the bills began to appear on the statement, which came to her parents' home. Her father thought the bills were obviously a mistake and wrote the credit card company, complaining.

When this father, a financial planner, found out what his daughter had done, he canceled her card—but not before she had allowed eleven thousand dollars to be charged on her credit card. It's no smarter to give a teenager a credit card without training than it is to give a baby a hand grenade. Eventually they will both discover what it was made to do, with about the same effect.

## Personal Expenses

The question is often asked, "Should we charge our children for their room and board if they are working?" This is a matter of judgment on the part of the parents. In general, I believe you should not charge a high-school-age child room and board. However, the needs of the family must be taken into consideration. If a financial need exists, it may be necessary for teenagers to contribute to the family's income. I have seen many such situations and rarely witnessed a detrimental effect on the child. In fact, usually the exact opposite is true, and the teenager reflected maturity far beyond his or her peers.

A widow named Pam was left with three children ages ten, twelve, and sixteen when her husband committed suicide while suffering terminal cancer. Because of the suicide, his insurance was voided, and she received virtually nothing. She had a few marketable skills, so she took up sewing at home. Her daughter, a high-school junior, got a job in the school office during weekdays and a job baby-sitting on weekends.

By her senior year, she had moved from the school office to a local attorney's office as a part of a school-work program. He was so impressed by her maturity and work ethic that he sponsored her to go to a court stenographer's school when she graduated from high school.

She later did all of his personal courtroom reporting and was earning a salary in excess of twenty thousand dollars a year. Within three years he had helped her to start her own transcription business, and at twenty-four she was managing an office with four transcription secretaries. She matured through her problems. Unfortunately, not all teenagers do.

Even with children who are out of school and working while living at home, the decision about charging them room and board is not simple. In great part, it will depend on the needs and attitude of the child. Even if the parents don't need the money, I believe it's a good practice to charge working children. They need the accountability that paying their own expenses can provide. You can always put the money in a savings account and give it back to them later when they move out on their own, if you wish.

## Adult Decisions

Ideally what we would like to achieve with our children is to totally prepare them to make the financial decisions they will be facing as adults. But most of them won't be trained to make decisions such as which house to buy, what type of life insurance to purchase and how much, etc.

The best way to prepare them, outside of actually buying those items, is to simulate the needs. In other words, do role-playing in which they make decisions similar to those they will make on their own. I have done this many times with high school classes where I would pair kids into teams to learn basic financial planning. I assign each team (usually a boy and girl) a job and related salary. For instance, one team is a schoolteacher making fifteen thousand dollars annually; another is a dentist making thirty-five thousand dollars; another is an assembly-line worker making twenty-three thousand dollars; another is a two-income family making sixty thousand dollars.

Each team is required to select the items for each area of their budget—from houses to vacations—with the applicable costs, such as down payments, monthly payments, utilities, and repairs. Their task is to fit what they select into their available funds each month.

After just one week of budgeting, most teams are looking to trade in houses, cars, clothes, and vacations—all in light of how much they cost compared to available funds. By about the fourth session, they become seasoned budgeters. With your children, find a system that works and use it.

ᴥ ᴥ ᴥ

Among the outcomes of Larry Burkett's experiences with students are two new books, each of which includes twelve lessons on

money management for youngsters, plus a thirteenth on the art
and grace of giving: First is *Surviving the Money Jungle,* for junior
high school students. Second is *Get a Grip on Your Money,* for senior
high. Both are published by Focus on the Family (Pomona, California: 1990). If you have children or grandchildren of these ages,
don't overlook these books! They will save you years of anguish
and help *you* as an adult, too.

In our fifty-two years of working with families and children who
needed financial counsel, we have never found a family or person
who regretted taking deliberate and determined steps toward
sound family management. This particularly applies to Larry's systematic approach. This chapter would not be complete without
passing on his ideas about how much of your income you might
spend on each standard cost-of-living item. These figures will vary

| Table 1 Percent of Income Spent for Standard Items | |
| --- | --- |
| Housing | 30% |
| Automobile | 15% |
| Food | 16% |
| Insurance | 5% (Life/disability) |
| Entertainment/recreation | 7% |
| Clothing | 5% |
| Medical/dental | 5% |
| Miscellaneous: Toiletries: Razor/shampoo/toothpaste Cash to carry Lunch money Gifts | 5–7% |
| Savings | 5% |
| Debt (Other than house/car) | 5% |

with family situations, yet they are experienced landmarks (see Table 1).

Remember that some of life's most valuable lessons are learned because of trying and failing. Love your children enough to allow them occasionally to come short of your expectations while they're still in your home. See that they have the benefits of this professional guidance and watch them mature in principles and methods of management in their own lives and eventually in their own homes.

# THREE

# VALUES: HOW MUCH ARE YOU WORTH?

E very Saturday night was our big time of the week when Dad took us kids to downtown Glendale, California—five miles south of our rural Montrose home—for our time on the town. On those nights we spent an hour or two mostly in five- and ten-cent stores like Kress' or Woolworth's when you could buy something for a nickel or a dime. Those nights were also times for lessons in values. And no home does very well whose values are not pretty well in hand. In those days, the lights of Glendale were as bright as Hollywood's, and how we liked those lights! We didn't do much shopping, but we looked, wide-eyed. How we ached to handle those counter items which seemed to be placed out there to tantalize kids! But Dad's rule was absolute: We must have cardinal respect for things that are not ours. *"We never touch anything that we don't plan to buy!"* he said.

Even though he wasn't great on *saving* money, over the years Dad's lessons in values expanded to include greater things like generosity, integrity, thoughtfulness, and many specifics in which he taught us through clear principles to deal rightly with people, and he set a sterling example. These included gender courtesies, language, penmanship, clothes, music, and table manners. We

47

start with *principles*, for in the first place they are the basic reasons why we have values—the basic *whys* of life. And when principles are put in the second or last place—sacrificed to *expediency*—you can be sure that you are living in a dying family, society, *or nation.*

## The Principle of the Thing

Dad got down to principles quickly. Behind every rule was the big principle that explained the why for the smaller rules: It was *The Golden Rule—to do unto others as we would have them do unto us.* (See Matthew 7:12.) Dad explained how storekeepers had to keep everything clean and in order on their notion counters so that they would be attractive to buyers. He observed how little fingers of many curious children could soil items and sometimes put them back in the wrong places.

Many people talk about principles, but few seem to understand that, good or bad, they are the reasons for actions. When we speak of "an act of love," notice the "of"; we are saying that love is not the act, but the principle behind the act, or in other words, the reason for the act. The same can be said for such principles as hate or dependability or indifference, and for everything that follows in this chapter.

People can become soiled by thoughtless passersby when the golden rule becomes impersonalized and when values become translated into bad habits and manners; on the other hand, they can be uplifted and inspired by even the smallest act of thoughtfulness. Two or three stories might help us get a clearer view of how values and manners, negative and positive, enter into the management of our lives.

Our friend Virginia Remick tells a people story about indifference and respect of younger for older: The little old man's hair was long and uncombed. His face had that drawn look that you often see on skid row, his eyes weary, almost teary, as he sat at the counter of a small town coffee shop. He seemed to have lost his last friend. The waitress had seen his type before and reacted typically, serving him with cold indifference, without a word of greeting or concern about what he might prefer.

He ate in silence.

When he finished, he moved toward the cashier, fished belaboredly in his pocket for a few coins to pay for his food and was turning to leave when an incoming customer glanced at him, took a second look, and blurted out excitedly, "Why you're Jascha Heifetz, the great violinist! I never ever expected, ever, to meet you," he effused, "much less see you here, of all places!"

The tired-looking man nodded and continued toward the door. Shaken, the waitress ran after him in obvious concern and remorse. "Oh, Mister, if I had only known you were *somebody*, I would have been friendlier."

"Madam," Heifetz looked at the waitress for a long moment and replied very quietly, "*Everyone* is somebody." And he walked out the door.

Our second story, coincidentally, is about a home-educated boy violinist, Ben Hames, and another violinist he *did* recognize. We found it in the Newsletter from Homeschoolers Australia, Ltd., and it tells something about respect—and encouragement—of older people for the younger:

> Ben was 'busking' [improvising on a set of harmonics] with his fiddle at Manly for the first time in months. The crowds were good, and he managed to earn his usual rate of sixty dollars an hour. Not unusual, you might think. Suddenly Ben was aware that he was being filmed by a television crew, again not particularly out of the ordinary.
>
> But then an old man leaned over close to Ben and gave him three dollars. Ben stopped playing to say thank you. As he looked up . . . his mouth fell open in utter amazement. [It was] . . . none other than Yehudi Menuhin [another home educated chap who became the world's greatest violinist of his day].

The third story tells something about respect of adults for adults. It was first told me by Dr. Charles Stokes of the University of Bridgeport a few years ago and, as I write this, the details are filled in by one of the confronters—himself.

It started one morning in 1951 when a "great big bear of a man in an old hunting jacket and several days growth of beard" barged into the office of Jo Studwell, veteran secretary to President Henry W. Littlefield of the University of Bridgeport, Connecticut.

"I wanta see the president," he blurted out.

Momentarily taken aback, yet always protective of her longtime boss, Miss Studwell dutifully performed her "He's unavailable" act, reinforced by Dr. Littlefield himself who stood behind the slightly-open door—but out of sight of the "intruder"—signaling to Miss Studwell to "Get rid of him!"

She was beside herself. Glancing toward President Littlefield's door, she noticed that he had stepped back so as not to be seen, so she heroically stood up to block the way between the big bear and her boss.

"Tell the president I want to see him," the big one barked again.

Dr. Littlefield, anxious to avoid a scene, came to the door as a first stage of his plan to usher the "intruder" out. He later told me about it himself.

But, said Dr. Littlefield, the big man was not easily moved.

"I want to see you," he bellowed with the authority of an old-fashioned New York lawyer.

Dr. Littlefield retreated into his office, this time reluctantly taking his "guest" with him and again leaving the door ajar.

A few minutes later President Littlefield gently closed the door, a practice he indulged only for confidential meetings and for very important persons, and signaled Jo Studwell that he did not want to be interrupted. To her wonder and puzzlement, the two conversed for over two hours.

When Dr. Littlefield finally emerged, he was talking like an old friend—with Charles Anderson Dana, the eminent New York lawyer and founder of Ohio's giant Dana Corporation, the multi-billion dollar manufacturer of auto parts and of New York City's Dana Foundation. "And," says Charles Anderson Dana University Professor of Economics Charles Stokes, "I can see evidence of the outcome of that meeting clearly today through my office window in science and classroom complexes, not to mention several endowed professorships which witness to the millions of dollars that 'old bear of a man' gave through the years."

Dr. Littlefield, who related details to me as we write this chapter, was soon vice president of the Dana Foundation, later headed it for a number of years, and is still a director. "You would never know Mr. Dana had a dime," he told me. "He never was offensive, but he was always simple and practical in his tastes. He liked to have Mrs. Littlefield pick up some sandwiches at a delicatessen and stop for a picnic along the side of the road. I had to take special precautions to insure that this sometimes ill-clothed man 'wandering' around classrooms and dining hall was not thrown off campus by our security. He lived very simply, but he was never tight."

## Mutual Respect of Children and Parents

It almost goes without saying that the person who does not respect others, regardless of age, race, color, creed, or national origin, will usually be one who has little self-respect. His irreverence or disrespect for others usually starts in early childhood by his own parents' lack of respect for him. Too often parents are preoccupied with their own wants and fail to respect the young child's need for parental warmth and responsiveness which cannot be satisfied with custodial care only. Few mothers and dads seem to understand that the earlier they institutionalize their children, the earlier their children, in their own minds, will institutionalize them. They do not realize that basic values are formed largely within the first twelve years.[1]

Such children in any given family have little genuine concern for their home and its needs for honesty, order, cleanliness, and economy, and are seldom promising candidates for managing their own families or businesses. Parents are the predetermined measures of the way homes are managed and the quality of products that family businesses produce. A well-managed family or family business has a well-defined, singular standard of excellence much like a piano tuner who pitches every instrument that he tunes at A-440, or he won't be in business long.

Let's try a couple of well-managed homes, one old-fashioned and the other up-to-date, to take a look at children and how they relate to their parents. See if time alters principles.

When I first visited Dorothy's home in Artesia, California, a year or two before we were married, I had some feelings in the pit of my stomach. What would her folks be like, particularly her father, Nels Nelson? They must be pretty good people, I reasoned, to have a daughter like Dorothy. But I also knew that they were conservative Norwegians originally from South Dakota and only a generation away from the old country. That uncertainty was settled very quickly. Mr. Nelson treated me, a mere fledgling, like any man he respected.

I quickly learned several things. First, the whole pattern of the Nelson's lives was consistent; this gave me a sense of security. Second, Mr. Nelson was a builder of quality houses; that relieved me even more, for I could talk with him on his own terms from my experience with my father. I have found such breadths of experience to be one of the great outcomes of family industries. And third, I was impressed with his integrity. He was scrupulously accurate and honest in everything he said and did, yet he had a friendly sense of humor.

Dorothy's mother was another story, one that seemed perfectly to complement her dad. Born Millie Amundsen and trained as a teacher in an old-fashioned "normal course," she never worked outside her home after she gave birth to the first of her four children. She helped her farmer husband, Nels, and fed threshers with her homemade and homechurned bread, butter, and apple pie.

When the Nelsons fell on hard times, she raised chickens and garden produce which she traded for staple groceries and fruit. Then she canned fruit and vegetables for winters. Dorothy recalls taking a pail down to the dairy where you could buy it much cheaper "flowing right off the refrigerated pipes" than having it delivered on your doorstep in quart bottles (as most did in those days before the advent of home refrigerators). She says that, like the Moores, even though they tightened their belts, they never knew they were poor. They always had enough to eat and were attractively and warmly, if not fashionably, clothed.

Dorothy and her sister learned to respect their mother and to learn her industry and careful home management. They came early to the conscious conclusion that they were much more fortunate than many of their girl friends whose mothers did not teach them how to cook, sew, and handle money wisely. "We had the best home economics course two girls could possibly have," Dorothy now recalls.

## Instilling Values

And this spirit is still here today. One of the clearest contrasts with today's unprincipled primrose path for so many families is the Christian safari of the McKims—their hunt for the best ways to build values systems in their brood of ten children spread over more than twenty years.

Julie is no washed-out, haggish old lady, but one of those rare, ageless Texas beauties whom you would never believe had a twenty-two-year-old university daughter. This high-school-educated but highly-learned mom wrote us in 1987 about how she and her truck-driver husband (who knows a lot besides trucks) were worried about the public school influence on several of their children.

"They were doing very well," Julie wrote, " . . . yet we were not seeing many of our goals accomplished in their lives." The McKims were concerned particularly about their youngsters' values and their need "to experience joy and motivation in learning without undue pressure, to expose them to special adults with much to offer them, and to experience a variety of situations otherwise not available."

About that time, Julie says, they received a book from Dr. James Dobson, well-known radio psychologist and best-selling family author. It was our *Home Grown Kids,* which she generously called "an answer to prayer for us, direction-wise." [2]

In 1985 they

began home education with all of our children. . . . Melisa had
done well in her year at Baylor University, but came home with
us as well as added to her transcript at a neighboring college.
She is now also involved in an apprenticeship situation with First
Baptist, Dallas, in their home school department, a position
which has never previously been offered to anyone without an
education degree. She is planning to obtain her CPA certifica-
tion. Melody will graduate from high school this year and further
her studies in music. Ken is a junior and desires to become an
attorney. . . .

Many of our successes are not measured by testing. Our boys
had the privilege of observing a nationally-known knee surgeon
in his office and also in surgery—scrubbed up and at his elbow,
looking through his teaching instruments. Our children have enjoyed many such special situations which would not have been
available to them through conventional means. A retired friend
taught these same boys woodworking skills that made them more
proficient than most grown men in several areas.

We have developed home businesses that have gained at least
thirteen thousand dollars in net income over the last seven months
[in addition to Mr. McKim's income; and this figure over a year's
time exceeded twenty thousand dollars]. Our children have been
very involved in all aspects of these businesses—crafts, baked items,
weddings (flowers, food, decor), new construction cleanup, and
speaking and singing for which we have been paid. . . .

Here again is mutual respect in action. The education of both
the old-fashioned Nelson tribe and the up-to-date McKim youngsters was, and is, in the final analysis, far more practical than it is
academic, yet typical of those who practice the work/study balance,
they excel in both. Among the values they and other working students learn are a few that may seem a bit obscure by today's educational standards. We discuss these in more detail in chapter 9.

## Money

Many of you will recall the story in our book, *Home Grown Kids,*
where Patty Spielman heard the toilet flushing on and on one day
while she was baby-sitting her granddaughter, "Pisha" (little Patri-

cia), age four. When Patty's curiosity finally led her to the bathroom, she wished that she had gone there much sooner, for Pisha was sitting calmly by the toilet with Patty's purse, flushing one hundred dollar bills down the sewer. When Patty asked, "What on earth are you doing?" Pisha's values and maturity were as clear as currency is to a four-year-old. She replied simply, "Well, Mommy says money is 'icky'."

A few weeks before this writing, on Christmas night in Montclair, Virginia, when we were sitting around the piano singing and telling stories, I wanted to give our grandkids a lesson in values. I held my index finger up to my lips and asked Bryon and Brent, nine and seven, not to say a word; then I called Bradd, three, over and made him an offer. In my left hand I had a bright 1989 penny; in the other a hundred-dollar bill. I asked him to take his choice. He wasn't sure, which was a sign of unusual maturity at that age. Most three-year-olds quickly take the penny. Then I sweetened my left hand offer with two more bright pennies. He unhesitatingly chose the three cents over the hundred dollars. Bryon and Brent roared. They suddenly realized the significance of *their* maturity.

Next I turned the tables on Brent, seven. I asked him to make his choice of a hundred-dollar bill or a twenty-dollar gold piece. He quickly said he would choose the hundred-dollar bill, knowing that a hundred is five times twenty dollars. But here a set of values of another kind emerged: He was unaware that such a coin was worth hundreds of dollars more than its face value.

Such variations in values are all around us here and abroad. In the mountains and in the desert a four-wheel drive truck or van usually has a much higher resale value than in Central Chicago. When, during World War II, I visited tiny Wari Island, off the southern tip of New Guinea, the natives gladly traded beautiful carved canes and spears or rare shell collections for loaves of bread or a bottle of peroxide to bleach their hair. And near Lae one day, a young woman offered her tiny daughter for a stick of black tobacco; little girls were not given much value in her tribe.

When I told her I didn't have any tobacco, she offered her child for a loaf of bread.

Such a trade sounds absurd on the face of it, and we quickly blame their "state of civilization." But are we any more civilized? Is it possible that we adults ultimately have about the same code of values, given the way television, sports, and personal convenience keep us from spending our time freely and constructively with our own children?

Growing out of the hundred dollar bill experience with Bradd and the gold piece question with Brent came a visit to the bank— an excellent exercise for young children in developing serious fiscal responsibility. My daughter Kathie took the boys to their Military Credit Union where they learned to make out deposit slips and about interest rates. Their questions ran something like this:

"What if the computer goes down?"

"There are some things we can do by hand such as cash a check in an emergency, but otherwise we just have to wait until we can get it up again."

"Does the bank ever run out of money?"

"Not really, but almost, sometimes."

"What do you do if you should run out?"

"We order some more from the U.S. Treasury."

"May we see your vault?"

"Yes, from the outside only, unless you have a safe deposit box. Then we let you in."

They also found how interest rates varied, depending on the amount of money deposited and the length of time it remained in the bank. Already much more responsible in the handling of their money, their next requested adventure was to visit the U.S. Treasury.

Dr. Robert Moon tells about his children's personal values. Bobby, the older, and not a CPA, liked to use the large car until he found that he had to pay for the gasoline for his private trips. At that point he decided to ask for the Volkswagen diesel. Jimmy, on the other hand, had second thoughts about taking a test for a driver's license when he found that he would have to pay the increase in the insurance premium. Granting authority can be a great way to build children and in particular to help them develop self-discipline, but only when you require them to accept commensurate responsibility!

Now back to Bradd and the hundred-dollar bill and shiny pennies: Was he really immature? Indeed. But not for his age since he isn't yet called to make major financial decisions. Adolescents and adults do much worse than that every day. They make decisions about tobacco, alcohol, drugs, and risk both physical and mental health permanently by promiscuous sex. We are hardly shaken any more when we hear of men and women candidly living together out of wedlock.

Even reckless eating demonstrates a far more serious state of immaturity in values than Bradd's. Indifference to things that are good for you inures you to the consequences which you will inevitably suffer. Like gold rushers in the 1800s who ended up in poverty because they couldn't tell the difference between iron pyrites, "fools' gold", and the real thing is the child or adult that doesn't learn that the price of living is to sacrifice present pleasures for future benefits.

## Common Courtesies

This principle governed all manners. I often wondered how Dad kept peace so well in a lively family of six children, three of them by my mother who had died when we were very young and three by our second mother. His code was thoughtfulness, and it ran through all family behavior. He was a strong-minded man, but never did we hear a harsh word to our mother. As for us, he borrowed from one of his favorite authors, insisting that our language must "be pure and kind and true, the outward expression of an inward grace." Kindness in no way conflicts with firmness, when that quality is needed. Words twice considered are far more worthy than thoughts quickly spoken.

Often in our anger or thoughtlessness we wipe out opportunities for advancement or peace, when a little patience or kindness would refresh all about us and cause the sun to shine through clouds which otherwise press upon us. Have you ever seen anything more beautiful, encouraging, or poignant than the sun's sharp, well-lined rays exploding through a break in the clouds? You and I can be that break.

An employee, for example, may ruin his chances for a raise by complaining about how badly he and his fellow employees have been treated. A well-mannered employee would discreetly ask for an increase, indicating his determination to apply himself even more diligently and efficiently in his work and help to keep overhead expenses down.

## Clothes and Such

I took clothing pretty much for granted and had little trouble in the old days as a teacher, principal, or city school superintendent with careless or suggestive garb. But in the late 1950s, just before the hippie era, some of us noticed an emerging carelessness about dress which ushered in an age of incorrigible defiance in schools.

An English teacher in a Buffalo, New York, high school was so distraught by the trend—with its tight trousers and shorts, miniskirts and sweaters without blouses or bras—that she discussed it with her senior English classes. Class members both wrote and spoke to other classes and came up with the idea of Buffalo's Magic Mirror, augmented by a series of student-made rules: For all boys, well-fitted, clean, pressed trousers with shirt and tie and either sweater or unmarked jacket; for girls, modestly fitted below-knee skirts and blouses (with bra where needed) under sweater or jacket. Full-length mirrors were set up at heads of stairways. The turn around in behavior and achievement was almost instantaneous.

Then in the early 1960s I learned another lesson. American Airlines offered free Admiral's Club memberships to VIPs. These airport lounges, also offered by United and TWA at the time, made travel much more convenient and provided a no-cost place to have small business meetings. If you were a congressman or college president or similar type, you were invited. I happened to be a college president and was thus honored. When I read the rules, I noticed that all men using the club had to wear a sweater or jacket. No exceptions.

One day I was signing in by the counter when a big, burly, carelessly dressed man entered the Los Angeles Airport Admirals Club. When the attendant reminded him of the rules, he heehawed. She wouldn't argue but quietly phoned the police. Shortly he was evicted. We have noticed similar rules in many stores and clubs—no bare feet, no shorts, no tank tops, and so on, which may be motivating to our children.

I recently read in the *Wall Street Journal* about Bernice Philbin, the maitre d' of Los Angeles' exclusive Beverly Hills Hotel who refused a distinguished guest admission into her inner elite dining room, regardless of the guest's protests, for the lady was dressed in a tennis outfit.[3] No matter how exacting this may seem, it is comforting to know that there are a few individuals left with some standards.

And finally, one of IBM's lead marketers told us recently of his introduction to their program. He "had never been one much to dress up." But in a brief pre-counseling session, he was asked if he had a dark, pin-striped suit, wing-tipped black shoes, white shirt, and conservative tie. He had all but the shoes and allowed that he could get a pair within the two hours before the appointment. Without that ensemble he was told he "wouldn't have had a ghost of a chance at the job."

This of course does not mean that we should dress up for dressing's sake, yet if we want to be accepted in terms of business success, we do well to be neat, clean, and dressed in a way most acceptable to most of our clients. For children that doesn't necessarily mean coat and tie, but it does mean clean body and clothes and neatly-combed hair, along with a winning smile—the most effective add-on of all.

## Music Tastes

The same principles apply in much the same way as with clothes, both as to cause and effect. Music has a direct effect on the emotions and values of anyone, but particularly impressionable youth.

And the potential damage to hearing caused by listening to hard rock music is well established.

We have always enjoyed good music, including hymns, semi-classical, and even classical, although we haven't been particular devotees of the classics. Yet we did not realize the influence of these tastes on our children until we lived in Japan. One evening after listening to the foreign news station, a musical program came on. Before long Dennis went over and clicked the radio off. I was surprised, although I had not been listening. He said simply, "That wasn't good music." And indeed it was marginal. It was also a lesson to me on the importance of good music in the home.

## Gender Courtesies

When we think of helpfulness between males and females, we usually are concerned about thoughtfulness for our women, although we don't suggest that it is inappropriate for women to give thoughtful attention to men, and for brothers and sisters to exchange thoughtful acts, as my sister still does for us by bringing over a meal when we return from a long and tiring itinerary. In this book we are particularly concerned about mutual courtesies, for they lighten the load in a busy household, especially when parents and children are involved in a family industry, and very especially in behalf of our wives and mothers.

It may be just carrying a load of groceries in from the car for your mom or wife, or opening or closing the car door for her. It may be doing a particularly messy sink of dishes soon after she has scolded you for coming home late for supper without giving her notice and making her reheat a specially planned entree whose "best foot forward" depended on a fresh-out-of-the-oven trip. In our home we have found that our women appreciate having their shoes shined or their tennies washed. You may think it too much to expect to open the car door for wife or mother or daughter or other woman and to help her fasten her seat belt, or yet to sacrifice an evening TV show or Sunday afternoon football game to wax and polish the floors or even to do a washing. But we guarantee that it will give a big boost to your home management shares on the family stock exchange.

## The Rewards of a Value System

Or it may be the positive, businesslike, and usually effective gesture of offering your children more authority in your home, reminding them of course that authority is delegated in proportion to the amount of responsibility accepted. This does great things for their mental health and yours, both immediately and eventually. When you put their names on the family checking account and ask them to keep accounts, to pay all the family bills, to do more of the family shopping, and to keep the home in generally good order and sound repair, these advantages at the least accrue these things to your home management program:

- They enjoy the thrill of authority—always a mental lift when it is properly delegated and accepted.

- They grow in dependability and creativity as they share responsibility for family duties which once burdened you.

- They relieve you to do other things, increasing your own efficiency and the likelihood of sounder family management.

- They generally move on to greater responsibilities and learn that work can be even more profitable and just as enjoyable as play; in fact, when done in the right spirit and with jobs that enhance their authority, and in their early years when done with you, such work (or chores, in some cases) becomes their highest form of play.

- They become more courteous and mannerly to you, their brothers and sisters, and to others around them, for in new responsibility, authority, and opportunities for constructively sharing in family life, self-respect now has its day. It is never born by idleness or indifference to others; on the contrary, it makes quarreling and faultfinding uncomfortable for both parents and children.

You collectively must decide what values are the most important in home management. If money is your first concern, you will
almost certainly have problems; but if sharing is your goal, your
solution of money problems will come much easier and will not be
so obvious when they do exist. As Dorothy often has said in her
lectures: "When we were victims, like others, in the Great Depression of 1929, we kids never knew that we were poor." It becomes a
lot easier to distinguish between wants and needs; in fact we then
find others around us more needy than we, and that is one of the
greatest rewards of a sound values system.

Many less than mannerly people are simply the victims of the
speed-up generations of the last fifty years and have no standards
by which to measure. Their parents haven't been around enough
or interested enough to live standards before them. They don't
know of men and youth giving women their seats on busses or
trains. They don't know that in any thoughtful society older people are treated with respect. They are indifferent to needs.

Good manners do often "get you somewhere." They may be
table manners, your patience at a pot-luck or smorgasbord dinner,
your gentleness when others are sharp, your willingness to ask appropriate questions when others are obviously opinionated.

Both Dorothy's and my parents taught us not to madly spear
our peas and beans with our forks. We were taught while yet very
young to be as quiet as possible and remember a little verse when
spooning our soup: "Like little ships go out to sea, I push my
spoon away from me." So we learned to tip our soup bowls away
from us, using our fingers on our spoon handles instead of grab-
bing them in our fists and digging them toward us. We were also
told to keep our napkins on our left knees, how to use knife, fork,
and spoon appropriately, and not to scrape our plates as if to destroy their surfaces. And among other things, we knew to clean up
our plates, yet not to fill our mouths too full nor try to talk with
bulging cheeks.

Sound silly? Perhaps some of these ideas are ancient, but the
ideals of self-discipline at our meals is one of the most important
of our mannerly activities, for we practice them day after day in all

kinds of company and all kinds of circumstances. We don't suggest formal dinner conduct at picnics. However, appropriate manners should govern all meals, even hit-and-run breakfasts. A thoughtful family is a genteel group, and in its own way a successful one.

## False Values

Dr. James Dobson once asked what I thought about his driving a Mercedes. I knew what he was thinking, for Dorothy and I had faced the problem time and again. Many years ago when one of our board members was a chairman of Ford Motor Company, Dorothy and I were offered a Lincoln Continental at a very low price—one which after six months we could have sold and made several thousand dollars. After thinking of possible community and constituency reactions, we turned the offer down. Some of Dr. Dobson's critics had commented on his red eight-year-old Mercedes diesel sedan which he had bought used at a very attractive price and which, because of that certain model at that time, was an excellent resale prospect. I told him that if immediate finances were the only consideration, he ought to keep it. Both of us knew, however, that the real question was quite different: Public-relations-wise, was it a good long-term business policy? He told me that he eventually sold it.

This doesn't mean that we justify every pastor and charity official who drives a Mercedes. We simply say that we do better to mind our own business and avoid pretense ourselves. If we are contributing financially to an operation, we may have a right to ask questions. But let's make sure they are the right questions. For example, recently a friend of ours bought a beautiful, low-mileage stretch limousine for eight thousand dollars from a charity to which it had been donated. It had cost nearly fifty thousand dollars less than five years before. What would you say after you arrived at church or a party in your family van if he drove up and parked by you? Would you narrow your eyes and speculate on his "extravagance?" Or with a broad-minded and generous outlook, would you see that he has a wife and five children to transport, including two that have to be strapped in children's car seats, and that if his garage is big enough, why not?

If you are particularly thoughtful, you may even think him pretty sharp. His limo cost less than half as much as your van and gets better gasoline mileage. Its quality is impeccable. In fact, you may wonder why you haven't done it yourself. Or would you?

At this point you face the *big* question: What really guides *your* values? Would *you* dare drive such a vehicle? If not, why not? If finances were the only consideration, would you? Would you be guided by principle or expediency? by comparative financial costs? by prejudices of your neighbors and friends? The answer, of course, depends on a lot of factors—your neighborhood, your garage size, your profession or trade, or possibly your own personal modesty or false pride or attitude in general.

But remember now, we are writing a book on home management and industries. To what extent will you allow your modesty or pride guide you in an otherwise honest transaction? In fact, many of our values, even among ostensibly moral, ethical, and religious people, are not sound at all. They are bound more by ego or convention—what others think—than they are by truth and sound management or relationship efficiency. Whether you drive a stretch limo or a van or a pickup truck becomes an important thing to think about.

Many of us have similar values about education, even tending to look down on those who do not have a set of college degrees. How stupid of us! Some of the grandest words of wisdom I have ever heard came from the proprietor of a country store; others, from a cement finisher with whom I worked.

A story was passed on to us about Franklin Meyer who during his high school years did most of the work on the family farm. This included caring for the chickens, feeding and cleaning up after the animals, milking the cows, raising and harvesting field crops and orchards, including twenty acres of apple trees. He was a leading athlete at high school and college and an acknowledged student leader, but as to values, he felt as he looked back that farm work had a stronger influence on his life than did school.

Finally, perfectionism can be one of the worst influences of all on sound management. Parents may think they have high standards, when they are actually overbearing and turn off any disposition their children have for helpfulness and efficiency. You may have to choose between an occasional extra dirty face or torn trousers on the one hand and happy cooperation on the other, especially if the dirt and tears didn't originate from presumptuous "sins."

You may have to put up with an occasional dirty dish when your husband or children clean up the kitchen, or some missed spots on a car-wash job if you share the job with your youngsters and seek their maximum growth and assistance in over-all management. They need time and space to grow. I find that I need it, too, and Dorothy's willingness to give it to me is one reason we are in our fifty-second year of marriage and have a reasonably well-managed home. She is also finding that if you are thoughtful and loving enough, you actually can teach an "old dog" new tricks.

So the word "values" is not necessarily positive. It is often characterized by envy, covetousness, selfishness, meanness, and jealousy. And your children are in enough danger from such social contagion from their peers to have to bear up with unreasonable (for their maturity levels) demands at home.

The best way to turn away the social cancer of peer dependency and values from your children, and to build positive socialization, is to be sure that you are spending much more warm, responsive time with them. If they are with you more than with their peers, making or doing things which interest them, they are much less likely to turn from family values.

Parents wonder why their children learn bad habits, manners, finger-signs, obscenities, rivalry, ridicule; why they participate in alcohol, drugs, sex, violence, delinquency, and occasionally even suicides. Too often their answer is in their mirror.

Whether children are schooled at school or home, their greatest potential influence toward a high value system is normally you, unless you are not a worthy parent. And whether they tell you or not, they cherish much more of your total devotion.[4] Otherwise they lose respect for you along with self-respect, optimism, and even trust in their peers; for they cannot even fully trust their peers unless they have a sound foundation of respect at home. And such foundations are only built by a lot of warm, constructive time together. Replicated research is crystal clear on this.[5] This is especially true up to their junior high school years or about age twelve.

This also happens to be the age by which children may be expected to develop adult-level perception and judgment—commonly called "cognition." [6] The key to this genuinely wonderful and helpful accomplishment is a great deal of warm educational responsiveness from you, enjoyable manual work with you daily to balance their studies, and simply being with you more than with their peers. Otherwise, don't expect them to be cognitively mature until between ages fifteen and twenty, with an average age of about eighteen. Early cognitive maturity can make a great deal of difference in a child's ability to accept responsibility, and so has considerable meaning in effective home management and industries.

## Know Thyself

The golden rule values system under your selfless parental guidance is an absolute condition of sound home management, for it demonstrates how honest you and your children are with others in the certainty that you will be only as honest with them as you are accurate in knowing yourself. If we kid ourselves along that it won't make any difference if we put something in our purses or pockets when we leave one of those "all you can eat (here)" restaurants, or if we give the motor officer a lame excuse when he picks us up for speeding, our consciences become more and more seared. We become caught up in situational ethics until eventually anything goes. The *Wall Street Journal* has published many investigative reports in recent years which show what eventually happens to such people when they carry such principles and practices into big business. Prisons, suicides, and societal and national decline tell the rest of the story. And our children learn from us.

On the other hand, the genuinely poised and mannerly child who combines integrity and dependability with hard work and high values is always in demand on the job and is an effective manager in your home. They may be mavericks by normal standards, but then who ever verified that it was best to be "normal?"

# FOUR

# THE WASTEFUL GENERATION

S ome years ago we received painful word from our niece, Linda Dixon, of serious water shortages in Marin County, across the Golden Gate Bridge from San Francisco. Linda was not in poverty. As a physician and American Board anesthesiologist, she and her family could be classed as well-to-do. But water shortages are no respector of wealth. Wasting water, like any other waste, lays responsibility squarely at all our doors, for nearly all of us are potential wasters in Western society. Waste management and prevention has become a key in sound home management. We are not sound managers in our homes if we do not share responsibility outside them. Our indulgence in running water, flush toilets, electricity, gas, telephone, or television puts us a notch above most of our world neighbors, and holds us heavily accountable for probable waste. We cannot preach a powerful conservation message unless we personally practice it.

Linda told us that eventually public officials rationed Marin households down to about forty gallons of water a day. On the face of it, this seemed absurd, for it didn't meet a tenth of their daily *wants*, but it had to meet all of their daily *needs*. They had to take "spit baths," limit toilet flushing, forget the dishwasher, lawns, gardens, and endless common uses.

## Water

We can hardly be comprehensive on this vast subject, nor is our purpose here to be offensively direct, but simply to take the long view in fairness not only to ourselves but also to our offspring and to our neighbors and nation. It may be onerous, even odoriferous, for example, to talk about toilets, but if we don't face up to our wastefulness, we shortly may have none to talk about. Many of us trip the flush handle at the slightest use. Linda and her family soon found frequent flushes, long showers, and running water in the sink a luxury, not a necessity. This makes particular sense when you multiply your savings by the thousands of families around you. With a little common sense and caution, many sections of America from southern California to New York City could have plenty of water where drought now threatens.

Lest this discussion seem below you, we remind you of the habits of royalty before the flush toilet era and their own indifference to the back yard privy. When we were shown around the famed Castle of Chillon on the shores of Lake Geneva, our guide observed that royalty simply used piles of straw for their relief, much like calving cows in our dairy pens. Then servants shoveled the excrement into the lake through an opening in the castle wall. Royalty weren't even as sanitary as old-fashioned farmers whose privies came about as close as any to the ancient Mosaic method of digging and burying, still widely used in communities around the world and by field armies.

In our seminars and books, many of you have heard our talk of sailor showers so common in the Navy. We told you of New Guinea days during World War II, when in that stifling, humid climate, officers and enlisted men alike were each given two gallons of cool water daily for showers: one to get wet before soaping and the other to rinse off. With rare exception, there is little excuse for our standing in our bathroom showers for fifteen or twenty minutes, or even ten or five, using twenty-five to a hundred gallons of heated water which frequently runs full force. Many parents find it both fun and productive to share with their children all this year's savings over last year's utility bills. Many find that the average cost of hot showers drops from fifty cents or more down to ten cents or even five.

Europe has set us an example in hotels and homes by using small hot water heaters at the kitchen sink or directly over the bathtub or shower, saving the water from having to course through cold pipes to warm them before warming us. These little units provide immediate hot water at low cost. Many American travel trailers now use similar units.

If we continue to be careless with our natural resources, we may find ourselves in the same predicament as crowded Japan, where during its years of hardship—and still in many areas—human excrement was diluted and used to fertilize gardens. Even now in many cities, the only water fit to drink is that caught from rain, or boiled, or purchased from markets, or delivered door to door by bottled water companies. Unless we are willing to be more careful and sacrifice present pleasures for future benefits, our children will one day have reason to curse us. So why not bend down that float arm or put two or three bricks in your tank so that each flush takes less water? Why not take shorter showers?

One other idea used by many hotels these days is the flow restricter in the shower head. Shower heads with restricters can be purchased for two or three to twenty dollars at your local hardware store or plumbing shop. For a few cents you can even buy a simple bib washer that fits your shower head and restricts the flow, and insert it yourself.

## Food

When we look at world starvation, we must view food waste as a crime. Nor does it make sense to place before our families the foodless food which so often mars our tables and destroys our bodies.[1] We refer also to refrigerator management and frugal preparation of food as well as to children whose parents give them—or let them take—more food than they should eat, and do not insist that they "lick the platter clean." And the poor and obscure are often as guilty as the rich and the famous. Most great religious leaders, regardless of faith, have bemoaned this kind of waste. Christ insisted that His followers "Gather up the fragments that remain, that nothing be lost" (John 6:12, KJV).

Waste from improper cooking, aging refrigerated foods, and unnecessary peeling of fruits and vegetables cost many families ten to twenty-five dollars a week, not to mention lost vitamins and minerals in the peelings. For example, nothing should be discarded from a head of celery. Tops, leaves, and outer stalks can be used in stews, roasts, etc., and lightly cooked and frozen in small quantities for later use. Likewise with broccoli, you will find that after you peel off the tough, woody outer part of the large stalks, you have a tasty morsel to use either raw or cooked. Tufts University's Diet and Nutrition Letter says that the stems and leaves are as nutritious as the florets.[2] And few vegetables can top broccoli in fiber content, not to mention its anti-cancer potential for lungs, bladder, and digestive tract.

Simply putting fresh vegetables in the refrigerator is not enough to retain their best quality. They need to be washed promptly and put in closed plastic bags, even in the hydrator; only tomatoes should be exposed in the refrigerator. I have often found a wilted, almost useless head of celery in someone's refrigerator, just as it came from the store, when it could have been crisp and delicious had it been properly cared for. For more on buying, cooking and caring for food, see our book, *Home Made Health*.

## Toiletries and Other Expendables

Few families have any idea how much they unnecessarily spend on everything from soap and shampoo to napkins, paper towels, and a potpourri of personal items. Keep a record for a year or make an estimate, and then make a deal with your children to cut down on waste. One family under financial hardship was using nearly a bottle of hair conditioner a week, not to mention expensive shampoos, lotions, creams, and an endless variety of pharmaceuticals. When one of the daughters mentioned that their grandmother used castile soap instead of shampoo and diluted vinegar instead of conditioner on her beautiful hair, the whole family was soon cutting their budget to the surprise of all. Vinegar, diluted one half or one part to two parts of water is much more effective than many so-called conditioners. Newly alert to the possibilities of saving, the family soon were diluting liquid soaps and rinsing out shampoo and soap bottles before discarding them.

In the next chapter—on recycling—we refer to waste of paper, yet we are tempted to remind you here of the excess usage of many adults and children of paper towels and toilet tissue, paper plates, and other sometimes wasteful practices. Several generations ago—and still practiced in some outlying areas—the Sears or Montgomery Ward catalogues always retired you know where. They were the poor man's (and sometimes the rich man's) toilet tissue out in the back yard privy.

Then there are grocery sacks. One old gentleman with old-fashioned values was recently given an award by a grocery chain for using one of its paper bags eighty-eight—yes, that's right, eighty-eight—times to take his groceries home. We are not only a prodical society in our demands for fancy packaging and endless paper and plastic products, but we destroy our environment with our excesses, as we will note in chapter 6.

## Buying and Caring for Clothes

It's no secret that clothes can weigh heavily on your budget, especially when picked out on a whim or of poor quality. Like a used car, the value of a dress or suit may be long gone the moment you take it out of the store unless the quality and fit are right and the garment has long term meaning to you. Quality is a key to sound management in clothing your family. Well-made garments and shoes more than reward you in comfort, wear, and self-respect. Sometimes we have found it an interesting practice to wear clothes longer and give new ones to those who had once received our used clothing.

One of our most interesting opportunities has been to give a lift to friends and relatives who once felt critical of us for being so conservative, but later found themselves in financial straits. Another has been the revelation that many habitually poor people buy in the most expensive grocery stores. One day while trying to help such a family, I asked why they did their buying at a certain store, knowing that its prices were high. They replied that the owner gave them credit until their welfare check came in. Their groceries meanwhile were costing them more than fifty dollars monthly than they should have been paying. We set out to show them how they could get on a cash basis with an even better quality of life and save where now they were losing.

If you operate on a small budget, as we have much of our lives, do you buy at so-called thrift shops or used-clothing boutiques? You may especially do well to visit church rummage sales in well-to-do communities, where discards are usually of high quality and in excellent repair. Here again you often see the well-to-do buying at these places, while the poor who need them most often ignore them.

And then there's that seeming providential, at least highly coincidental, happening which sometimes enters everyone's life, and we shouldn't refuse it. This last Christmas, Dorothy and I were puzzling over what to buy our grandkids. They have plenty of toys, we thought, and we have helped them get started in business by giving them the golf balls we pick up when we walk near a local golf course, and they in turn add to those they pick up and sell at a course near their home. We couldn't get one idea out of our minds. We never were much to buy pictures, but the three boys—nine, seven, and three—liked lions and tigers. But where would we find such old-fashioned things.

One day after an unusually bad wind and rain storm in the desert where we are writing, I passed a neighbor's open garage and noticed some pictures lying face down and scattered about on the concrete floor in sand and dust blown in by a heavy morning

wind. Since his car was gone, I stepped over and stood the pictures up against the sheltered side of the garage. Among them
were seven beautiful paintings and prints of male and female
lions and tigers, six of them framed and one very large wall piece
printed on cloth! As I was setting up the last one, our neighbor
drove in. "Would you like them?" he asked. "I've been trying to
give them to Goodwill, but they won't come." So the boys have
their pictures; we decided to send Goodwill a little cash, and everyone has a good deal.

There's a difference between scrounging and being selective.
Size, color, or style may be a problem, but be patient, shop around
and come back. The finest blazer I ever wore hung for weeks on a
rack in Newport Beach, California's tiny second-hand shop. I
found it after tripping down the yellow pages and making several
calls. Such shopping can be real fun, even exciting! For sixty-eight
dollars they sold me a four hundred and fifty dollar Navy-blue
blazer, virtually new, which fit as if it had been tailored for me. I
wear it almost every week. And I still use a princely vicuna overcoat
which I purchased for twenty-five dollars in 1951 at a Chicago's
North Clark Street used clothing area. We travel extensively in our
seminar circuit and must make a decent presentation on the plat-
form, yet our clothing budget is a small fraction of most of our
friends'. Even when we have gone to Goodwill or the Salvation
Army—usually to give something—we have occasionally lingered
to find good buys.

And carelessness in clothing care is one of waste's best friends.
Nor is it only children and old folks who decorate their ties and
blouses with drippings from their forks and spoons and toss their
garments at random on the floor or in the closet. I take simple
precautions when eating at home in my good clothes. It's called
an apron, and doesn't require a great deal of dignity. And on
planes no one yet has ridiculed or demoted me for tucking my tie
into my shirt and out of food's way or using my napkin as a bib.

Special care should be taken with clothes which must be dry-
cleaned or commercially pressed. We have often washed out just a
spot or two in an otherwise basically clean garment to postpone an

expensive over-all cleaning. Whether women or men, it pays to fold or hang clothes up in an orderly way. Why not have a place for everything and everything in its place? I have watched with amazement as travelers stash fine clothes into overhead compartments or racks on buses or planes. It takes little more effort to turn a blazer inside out, tuck one shoulder into the other, as a tailor taught me, and lay the garment gently on top in the compartment or rack. With high quality material and a little care, our cleaning bills and problems of wrinkling or disrepair no longer plague our budget.

## Shoes

Shoes, likewise, suffer far too much anguish. If they could talk, they would tell you, "Please, just take a couple of minutes to clean us up and give us a facial! Don't make us feel as if we were from the other side of the tracks." A handy shoe kit is an economical luxury. Make its intelligent use a habit. Then keep them in good repair by walking straight and not scuffing. My problem is a latent polio limp which I try to cover, but which cost me heavily in new heels until I found shoes—on special—made by French-Shriner, Nunn-Bush, and others that don't require re-heeling during the life of the shoe.

Shoes probably are the single most often misfits of all clothes. We like the style and price but forget how they might feel after we have walked in them a few miles. Soon they are suffering in a corner, grieving that we have rejected them or given them away, in either event a wasteful habit.

Some who are determined to brave out the agony of misfits eventually become cripples or pay out big sums to local podiatrists. This is especially true for women who have this thing about high heels and pointed toes, doing some painful thing in behalf of their pride. Dorothy says they accentuate shapely ankles. I have my own ideas about that. But what a price women pay in wrenched backs, impaired walks, and feet sometimes bound almost like the ancient Chinese.

Fortunately for me, after a few mistakes I talked with a wise shoe man. He noted that my toes were almost against the end of a pair of shoes I had selected and suggested that I should have at least a half-inch to spare. I mildly protested that I always wore 10½ D. "That's probably your trouble," he observed. "In the first place, all shoes aren't made on the same lasts, and second, you probably would do much better with the longer size 11 C." I couldn't believe him. I thought only of foot width, yet sure enough, 11 C was my size. In five minutes he saved unnecessary medical bills and painless walking ever since.

## Equipment and Toys

Carelessness in care of appliances, vehicles, tools, and toys is a drain on almost every family treasury. Some require more attention than others, yet with a little tender, loving care, the average family can save hundreds of dollars yearly. For safety's sake toys and tools should never be unnecessarily left lying around the house nor the yard. This orderly practice is for both adults and children, saving *mental* decay as well as the metal rust that goes with carelessness. If a toy or appliance needs repair, fix it soonest; however, *avoiding* damage is best of all.

Some of our svelte modern equipment is not as hardy as Grandma's old cast iron frying pan. Not long ago we invited a temporarily homeless family to use our home while we were on an extended speaking trip. When we returned, Dorothy's favorite Teflon skillet was marred beyond repair from someone scraping it with a metal spoon instead of non-scratch cookware. Some families "just love to have" nice china around, when something less breakable would be much less costly in money and stress. Just a chip or one broken dish mars a set—and usually somebody's feelings. All the more reason for selecting a pattern which can easily be replaced, if you are so fortunate as to have that privilege.

If any appliance with moveable parts makes a strange noise or smell, stop using it immediately and check it out thoroughly, lest your repair costs be multiplied. Common sense is one of your best management tools of all. A girl who stayed with us a while nearly destroyed our best vacuum cleaner by failing to empty it, and one day, like a balky, mistreated mule, it refused to work. The same young lady was splitting small logs on the overhang of our expensive marble hearth which the original owners had laid, smashing the edge to bits. She is long gone, but we still have the memorial to her thoughtlessness. Some of our best home management counsel says to use common sense, and if you have any doubts for servicing and use, first read the instructions.

## Recreation

Here, like appetite, most of us find it hard to change. As a former public school coach and sports addict, trained at the University of Southern California—one of America's foremost sports addiction coves—I found it extremely difficult to put sports in perspective as "recreation." This word means in essence an activity that rebuilds and recreates in a balanced way. How does that fit your recreational philosophy and practice? Well, it didn't fit mine. I had to reason through many times the idea that true recreation would in truth have to follow the golden rule and apply the 4-H concept in building head, heart, hand, and health. How does that fit with *your* philosophy? If it rings true, you are in good shape for the high personal quality of recreation which inspires, builds the 4-H's, reduces immediate and long-term costs, and makes you a self-controlled, all-around better manager.

Otherwise, reappraise the value and necessity of your recreational activities. How much time do you spend with TV, videos, and similar passive activity? How much money do you as a manager spend on events which you view passively but which are transient in terms of inspiration? How many of these genuinely educate or build? This is not to say that all passive recreation is unprofitable. A symphony, oratorio, or good book may offer both education and inspiration that last. However, I found that rivalry sports in a mature sense were costly in time, money, and wasted emotional energy. Many of our friends who say they do this to relieve themselves from stress seldom seem to be relieved, but often rather to be angered because a referee made a bad call and their team lost, or have lingered all week on the edge of their seats in anticipation of another win against an evil foe, or yet for a championship which builds nothing but ego and has no permanent meaning. It is intriguing to follow sports through history: You can't escape the conclusion that as families and nations—Chaldea, Medo-Persia, Greece, Rome—became increasingly devoted to sports and amusements, usually during prosperous times, their moral fiber disintegrated, and in a few generations they were defeated or destroyed.

Western society has gone far enough down that path of waste today to be reckless by any standard of the past: not only in food and time but in sheerest indifference to costs. The other day Dorothy and I were walking by a tennis club, not a fancy one, just a part of an average country club. We saw some tennis balls lying around after all players were gone; every one was firm and fuzzy, so nearly new that the names "Wilson," "Penn," and "Dunlop" were still there in clear, unworn black letters. So we picked them up and carried them over to a ledge by the office of our friend the tennis professional, thinking they had been lost. We mentioned them to him the next day, but his reply was, "We don't bother with those." One day we saw at least a dozen and a half discarded balls in the trash receptacle on *one* court.

## Things

If you would like a real, sometimes exciting, learning experience with your children, follow a trash truck around town. Or if you find that revolting, drive around your neighborhood on trash day and observe the vast variety of waste waiting for the big truck. Dorothy and I have seen lovely furniture, carpets, and odds and ends basking in the sunshine—or the rain—from Olney, Maryland, to southern California. We estimated when we lived in Hinsdale and La Grange, Illinois, that it would not take long to furnish a home quite comfortably, maybe even luxuriously.

Two of our nicest pieces are a once scruffy old adjustable rocker and a painted chest of drawers which were thrown away in Loma Linda, California. The rocker had been manufactured a hundred years before, and with a little refinishing and upholstering it became a prized classic which many have envied. Our daughter, Kathleen, stripped the chest, which turned out to be an antique treasure. There is more on this kind of thinking in chapter 9.

However, we would caution even here. With money being thrown around like dust these days and men and women bidding into millions of dollars for an old (or new) Ferrari, Rolls Royce, Lamborghini, Mercedes, Dusenberg, or Bugatti—and all the risks such "investments" entail—even classics and antiques should have their limitations.

## Vehicles

Automobiles, motorcycles, boats, ski-machines, even bicycles have cost many families heavily. We don't propose to lecture here on the virtue of dealing only with necessities, but a few cautions are in order on waste. Recently one of our close neighbors, a single mother, was having a problem getting her car started. As I remember, it was a recent model Toyota van, but was clanking loudly enough to wake up the neighborhood. When I went over to help, I found the engine's dip stick dry; it showed no oil at all. I asked her about the last time she had the van serviced, but she didn't remember if she had *ever* done it. The best she could figure, the van had traveled twenty thousand or thirty thousand miles without any attention to water, oil, battery, or tires. Recently divorced, she had always left such things to her husband.

Even a child's bicycle should have its weekly rub down. Such a massage job won't hurt your child; rather, it will develop his own dependability, pride, and self-respect. And every vehicle, large or small, should be kept under some kind of cover if possible. Add to this a weekly washing of your car and a coat of wax every few months, and your net profit in terms of value and staying power of your vehicle often amounts to hundreds of dollars yearly. If you buy a simple control nozzle for your garden hose and have a bucket of hot detergent suds, car washing is easy. Most of the drying may come from the heat of the water, if you rinse your car frequently. There are excellent waxes which require only an hour or so to apply and polish. If you don't know how to buy cars or where to have them serviced, seek counsel from several friends who are obviously successful with cars. Then proceed as though a misstep might break you up in business. It might! And it goes without saying that the interior of a car tells a clear true story of a person's basic habits.

## Time

Perhaps the greatest waste of all in a wasteful generation is our prodigal use of time. Time management is just as important to the success of our homes as it is to major corporations. We have already suggested that sports, amusements, television, idle reading, carelessness, and simple lack of understanding of the importance of time cause more waste than most of us know. If we parents and teachers were accountable only for ourselves, we might not be so heavily on the hook; but we are responsible by use of precept and example for the values of the next generation. If it doesn't survive, the implications of tragedy rest at our door or hover over our graves.

This week as I write this chapter, a clean-cut young mechanic is working on a nearby home. His principal concern these days is how to get ahead. He says he serves his church well, but he has no time for anything that gives him hope for his family's future. I asked if he had any college behind him. No. Had he planned on any? No. There was neither time or money. I asked if he knew that the time before midnight was worth two to three times that after midnight for productive sleep. No, he hadn't. I asked then if he knew that the time in the morning before breakfast had a value of three to five times as much for study as time after supper at night. No, again.

He shortly decided to call a major college's extension department on a toll-free 800 line, to obtain information on low-cost tuition at one of the finest schools in America, and to complete his college course studying early in the morning before he goes to work—as thousands are doing from New York University to Cal-Berkeley, including many church colleges.

Then there is the mother (or dad) who has six errands to run today and will take three or four trips to run them instead of one or two. She will go to one end of town and then retrace her route to the other end because she did not plan ahead of time to do her errands in the most time (and transportation) saving sequence. We offer more of this in chapter 7 on becoming organized. But the idea here is to take a little time now and then, early in the morning or after the children are in bed at night and let your mind run over the day to think how you could have saved time, then use your ideas another day.

Where possible in terms of money and storage space, Dorothy buys in bulk so that she doesn't have to go to the store often for common items. She tries to cut down the number of trips to market. There will always be emergencies, but with careful planning, every day need not be an emergency. We don't advise going overboard on bulk buying, for we realize that some items require frozen storage, others dry storage, and still others insect- and mouse-free storing; and storage often may be more costly than the extra trips.

## Air

It will seem futile in some cities to mention the possibility of clean air, nor will we say much about this most immediately vital of all nature's gifts. Yet, no matter how futile it may seem, it is time for all of us to lend our influence to keeping smog, haze, air-dirt, or whatever you may call it, from increasing, and to do all we can to reduce it. It is a personal as well as collective responsibility, and if the thousands who read this book step in and do their share, and encourage those already pioneering, it will be well worth the writing.

## Health

Those who are truly concerned about not wasting their health are up against one of the heaviest challenges to their self-control. Common sense seldom reigns in the things we eat and drink and the way we eat and imbibe, even in a day of health consciousness. And we pay a heavy waste bill in money, time, job advancement, and happiness. Poor health habits in eating, drinking, exercising, breathing, using sunshine, resting, and trusting are abuses of the mind as well as the body. But a body well used insures a mind unabused, creative, pure. Health, like time, is unique from other wastes, for they cannot be replaced as other things can. Yet both of them challenge us to sacrifice present pleasures for future benefits.

## Waste Reduction

Waste reduction is the prevention of wastes at their source by redesigning products or changing patterns of the producers and of us, the consumers. Unlike recycling, which we discuss in the next chapter and which involves the recovery of products from the waste "stream," waste reduction slows the flow of waste entering the waste stream.[3]

The amount of material discarded can be reduced through the following ideas.

### Product Re-use

Reusing products is as simple as donating or selling old household appliances or repairing products instead of discarding them. Used products can be donated to charitable organizations or resold through yard sales, classified ads, and flea markets. Consumers should buy reusable products and those that are bio-degradable as much as possible. Many stores are already using plastic sacks which will disintegrate within a relatively short time in garbage dumps or landfills.

## Product Durability

We can cut down on unnecessary manufacturing by buying products with longer useful lives. Household appliances that last longer and are repairable are readily available. *Consumers Reports* and similar publications *are excellent sources for such counsel. For example, automobile tires' average durability has almost doubled from fifteen thousand or twenty thousand miles to forty thousand miles with the replacement of bias-belted tires with radials.*

## Reduced Materials Usage

Reducing the amount of material used in a product means less waste when the product is discarded. Steel can manufacturers have in recent years reduced the weight of cans. Others are reducing material usage through redesign of both products and packaging. You and I can help in this effort wherever practicable by buying packaged items in larger containers, assuming we are not risking spoilage.

## Reduced Consumption

We can borrow or rent items which we would use infrequently. Renting tools and larger use of libraries through borrowing magazines and books are examples of good home management which reduces waste through savings on purchase, maintenance, and elimination.

## Recycling

Where it *is* necessary to buy and eventually dispose of a product, there is now available one of the most intelligent, practical waste-combatting efforts of our generation—recycling. You, with relatively little opposition or disappointment, may become a community leader and save both now and through the years. In the following chapter we will show you how you can both practice and lead in this remarkable development.

# FIVE

# RECYCLING: HAPPILY MAKING NEW OUT OF OLD

W e learned about conservation early in our married life during World War II when it was patriotic to recycle our cans, and to some extent the success of the war depended upon it. We faithfully washed those cans, removed the labels, tucked both ends inside the can, then stomped them flat to make them compact for collection. We still have that habit today; wherever there is a recycling center, we have saved reusable materials.

We remember well also being coached over the radio (there was no television in those days) on how to make bed sheets and soap (which, like sugar and gasoline, was rationed) last longer by washing only the bottom sheet each week, and rotating the top sheet (which is obviously cleaner) to the bottom each time. This was also before fitted sheets. Then when the sheets wore thin down the middle, as they usually do, we were advised to split the sheets down the middle, sew both edges together and hem the new edges.

And of course there was compost. Today the garbage man hauls our grass cuttings, garbage, cans, and waste paper away. Not

in World War II! Thus for the last nearly fifty years we have composted our garbage as well as lawn clippings. This has also taught
us to buy fewer newspapers and to cook more of our food fresh
instead of opening cans.

Still another suggestion returned us to using cloth napkins instead of paper. So once again we began using our napkin holders—one for each member of our family and for each guest who
stays with us for more than one meal. And we use few paper napkins or plates. It takes a few more minutes to wash the dishes, but
the process is considerably less expensive if we wash the dishes by
hand instead of running the full hot water cycle in the dishwasher.

Does this sound stingy? You asked for ways of saving and of
managing well, and that's the way it is. And if we sound picky, take
a lesson from Ralph Nader: One cold Michigan morning he came
over to our house for breakfast. When Dorothy tore a plastic wrap-
per off a book we were giving him, and tossed it into the fireplace,
he quickly remonstrated, pointing out that the burning plastic
would pollute the air. And he was right.

We stayed for several weeks with our children in the Virginia
village of Montclair, a few miles south of Washington, D.C., and
had our faith restored in society as we watched the makings of the
most mature and effective recycling program we have yet seen.[1]
And since writing this chapter, we read in the December 1989
*Guideposts* of a coincidental Montclair (New Jersey) that has a similar program. Michigan and other states have for many years cut
down on beer can litter by requiring five- or ten-cent deposits
which provide anti-litter incentives for buyers and which anyone
who picks up litter may redeem.

## Something to Think About

Who likes to think about waste or garbage, anyway? Yet that is no
longer an elective question. If we don't join those who are doing
something about it, we will one day drown in it. If you think this is
slightly exaggerated, imagine you were with us in beautiful Hawaii,
the Paradise of the Pacific, a year or so ago when the Honolulu

City trash disposal workers were on strike. Day after day, week after week, garbage and trash overflowed over sidewalks, streets, restrooms, and public buildings until in some places it formed veritable stench-filled mountains of refuse. Then we watched helplessly as the wind with devilish delight scattered the city's dregs over the streets and beaches until the residue of the city was its carpet.

Before we get into the remedies and business opportunities which recycling offers, we offer some insights which may help you make up your mind to read the rest of this chapter and book, and join one of the most vital movements in our nation.

- Every American, on average, generates approximately 1,788 pounds of garbage annually.

- Approximately eighteen thousand trees are required to publish one Sunday edition of a leading newspaper.

- Office workers are America's leading waste paper generators.

- Packaging takes over half of America's paper production, 75 percent of our glass, 40 percent of our aluminum, and 30 percent of our plastic. (You can imagine how wild this seems to old timers when only two generations ago we largely did without packaging for most grocery and hardware items, and what packaging there was, consisted of tin cans, glass jars, cloth sacks for flour, sugar, and salt, cardboard boxes for breakfast cereals, and burlap bags for potatoes and onions. You often brought your own sack for beans and always your own cardboard box or knit bag to carry the small items away. And you made dishtowels, aprons, and even children's clothing from your flour and gunny sacks for years.)

- Forty-eight billion cans yearly are discarded—196 cans per American.

- 1.96 billion pounds of bauxite are mined and refined annually to provide us with aluminum beverage cans.

- Enough trash and garbage is landfilled annually to bury twenty-six thousand football fields ten feet deep in garbage and trash.

- In ten years over half of American cities are expected to run out of landfill capacity.

- Disposing of wastes is the third heaviest tax burden on local communities. More than 4.5 billion dollars is spent annually to collect and dispose of America's waste.

- Recycling one aluminum can will save enough energy to keep a one hundred watt lightbulb burning for three and a half hours.

- Three cubic yards (eighty-four cubic feet) of landfill space is saved when we recycle one ton of newspapers.

- About one out of every eleven dollars spent by consumers goes for the cost of packaging.

- About three thousand tons of tin—an expensive metal which we largely import—are now recycled yearly in America.

- There is an energy saving of up to 30 percent by recycling glass. One hundred percent of used glass can be recycled into new glass.

- Four million tons of recycled paper is shipped abroad to foreign markets annually.

- Motor oil never wears out. It can be cleaned, reused as new oil, or further refined into gasoline or other products. The only appropriate way to dispose of oil is to recycle it.

- Forty-two gallons of high quality crude oil is used to make two and a half quarts of motor oil. One gallon of reused waste motor oil will produce the same amount of new motor oil.

- Most households replace a major appliance at least once every five years.

This chapter is a sort of test of our citizenship, of our concern for our children's future. We may be tempted to say that what we do won't make any difference, but that would be one way of destroying civilization, and long before we do commit collective suicide, police might be at our front door to see that we cooperate in a community program in which we should have been leaders.

As Christians we should bemoan our nation's status as the most wasteful nation in the world. God will hold us responsible for our use of the natural resources He has provided. The judgment includes a warning that he "shouldest destroy them which destroy the earth" (Revelation 11:18, KJV).

Prince William County provides residents of communities like Montclair weekly recycling bins where they store all glass and tin and aluminum cans after rinsing them. The bins are placed out on the curb with bundled newspapers on top of them in paper bags or bundled with twine for their weekly collection. The trash service sorts the materials in the bins into a special recycling truck. But first, the county and Montclair Village have carefully educated their residents on the program.

Here are some of their carefully worked out reasons and practices:

- Recycling can earn you money.

- Recycling can reduce your disposal costs.

- Recycling saves resources.

- Recycling saves energy.

- Recycling reduces the size of disposal sites.

- Recycling reduces litter.

- Recycling takes little time and effort.

- You can make twenty recycled aluminum cans with the energy it takes to make one new aluminum can. There are approximately twenty-three cans to one pound of aluminum.

- It takes three tons of recycled newspaper to make one ton of paper.

- Paper made from waste papers instead of virgin wood requires 61 percent less water and results in 70 percent less air pollutants.

- A foot of newspaper tightly twined equals thirty pounds.

- Sixty-six one-foot bundles of newspapers equals one ton.

- Eleven six-foot stacks of newspaper equals one ton.

- Nature can recycle a tin can to dust in one hundred years, and an aluminum can in five hundred years, but a glass bottle in one million years.

## Why Recycle?

Recycling materials instead of discarding them has always been practiced at some level. Today the world's resources are in danger of being exhausted, while consumption of these resources has continued to increase at an alarming rate. Increased consumption means increased waste. Every American discards an average of five pounds of material per day. As a nation we discard almost 250 million tons of solid waste annually. The way we are going now, the time is coming that when we empty the trash can, we won't be able to throw it away, for there will be no "away." One way to prolong our resources is by recycling. After reducing our discards to a minimum by reuse of materials, we should recycle what we *do* discard.

### Recycling Conserves Energy

One ton of aluminum from ore requires sixteen thousand kilowatt-hours (sixteen million watt-hours or four-hundred thousand forty-watt light bulbs burning for one hour), while one ton of aluminum from recycled metal only requires 187 kwh. Recycling of other household discards such as paper, cans, and glass all contribute to energy conservation.

### Recycling Saves Natural Resources

The possibility of today's landfills being tomorrow's metal mines is no longer laughable. Ore deposits throughout the world are being rapidly depleted. Much of America's metal ore needs are supplied by other nations. Continual recycling and reuse will do two things: delay depletion of our resources and decrease our dependence on imports, a stark concern nowadays. Furthermore, recycling one ton of paper saves seventeen trees. Many industries producing products from recycled materials cause less air and water pollution than industries producing equivalent products from raw materials.

## Recycling Helps Solve Solid Waste Problems

Much, if not most, of our solid waste ends up in landfills. Among the many problems is leachate which is formed when water percolates through waste, picking up contaminants. This eventually pollutes surrounding land and water for many years. Now landfill space rapidly is filling up, and replacements are so hard to find that last week's news reported that the U.S. government is considering using the Marshall Islands as a dump.

While recycling will not eliminate the use of landfills, it does result in longer landfill use for non-recyclable materials. Recycling is only one step in handling waste, but it is so important that we should all work together, for we have only one earth.

## What to Recycle?

### Glass

Reuse glass containers wherever possible, including canning, storing, and decoration. Watch for beverages which are sold in returnable containers and are significant contributors to both energy and waste saving. Otherwise glass for recycling should be washed and all metal caps and rings removed to be separately recycled with metals.

### Paper

Recycled paper is classified into a number of grades:

*Newsprint.* Any newspaper which is not bound by a glued edge is recyclable. Newsprint is often the largest part of waste from a household and is the easiest to recycle. About 12 percent of America's waste is newsprint, yet currently only about 2.5 percent is recycled. It merely needs to be stacked and tied both ways in manageable bundles or slipped into large paper sacks. Your recycled newspaper will show up in such products as insulation, packing materials, fiber pipes, roofing materials, and newspaper. Corrugated, chipboard, and kraft papers make up to 50 percent of the paper produced in America. When recycled they are made into similar products.

*Corrugated cardboard.* This has two layers of heavy cardboard with a ribbed section in between and is commonly used for heavy-duty cartons. Plastic coated or tar-lined materials are not recyclable.

*Chipboard.* Here we have a thin, gray-colored cardboard used for cereal boxes, tablet backings, and paper rolls. It is of a lower grade than corrugated and often recycled as scrap paper.

*Kraft paper.* This is a brown paper used in grocery sacks and wrapping paper. It is often recycled with corrugated board, but check with your recycling center first.

*High grades.* There are three types of hi-grade recyclable materials: computer paper, tab cards, and ledger. On the household level, most often ledger is collected. This includes typing, mimeo, notebook, ditto, and writing paper. Plastic or wax-coated, carbons, cellophane, newspaper, and glossy magazine paper must not be included. At the recycling plant high grades are shredded, repulped, de-inked, and then remade into bond paper, tissues, and wrapping paper. When you ask for recycled paper you naturally increase demand for this product.

*Scrap.* This final category of paper includes all types not previously mentioned. Most of it is found in packaging. Perhaps 47 percent of all paper is produced for packaging. The incident of tampering with self-displays has demanded increased packaging to help insure safety for the consumer. The more we package, the more paper we obviously consume, and the more potentially we waste and destroy our environment.

Magazines provide another source of scrap paper. They are more difficult to recycle because of their high clay content which gives them their shiny appearance. The best way to recycle them is to share them. It is not out of the realm of possibility that one day we will have no more glossy magazines.

Scrap paper is not yet in demand as a recycled product, but it does find its way into such uses as egg cartons, chipboard, and roofing materials.

## Metals

*Tin cans.* These are typical food cans. They should be washed out, ends and labels removed, and the can flattened. When recycled, the one percent of tin in the cans is removed and the 99 percent steel is recycled as scrap. Tin is a scarce resource that should have priority in our recycling.

*Bi-metal.* These are usually beverage cans—tomato juice, orange juice, etc. They often have pull-tab openers, steel-seamed sides and aluminum tops. The top should be removed and recycled separately from the steel portion of the can.

*Aluminum.* You will notice that all-aluminum cans are molded without seams. They are soft with a rounded base and indented top. To recycle them, merely rinse and flatten. Any other aluminum items such as TV dinner and foil pie plates should be kept separate from aluminum cans because of differences in grade.

*Other metals.* All scrap metal such as pipe, appliances, and sheet metal is recyclable. Other materials such as copper wiring and lead from batteries are also recyclable and have a high resale value.

## Other Materials

*Plastics.* Most household plastics are recyclable. Yet plastic still is difficult to recycle. Many centers will accept beverage bottles which they bale and ship for grinding and using in filling for sleeping bags, making fish line, etc.

*Oil.* Motor oil never wears out; it only gets dirty. This can be drained and taken to the nearest oil collection center. It is then shipped to a refinery where the impurities are removed and it is marketed as re-refined oil or as industrial fuel oil. This is one of the most important of our recycling processes—preventing it from ending up in the ground or in our waterways.

*Organic wastes.* Kitchen garbage and similar organic wastes and lawn trimmings comprise about 18 percent of Prince William's waste. It can often be used at home to enrich the earth through composting. This is a controlled decaying process. We use this in our home for our garden. It does not result in a smelly garbage pile that attracts flies, if properly done. We usually cover our garbage with grass from our lawn or leaves from trees which we keep in a nearby pile. Soon worms make their way through it, and it becomes a rich humus. When we carefully dig compost into the garden soil, our production exceeds that of our neighbors who use chemical fertilizer.

## How to Recycle?

Recycling should begin at its source: your home. If you put everything first into a garbage container, you contaminate recyclable materials. If you think this takes too much time, look at the findings of the Environmental Protection Agency: The total social inconvenience to the average householder is seventy-three minutes and two cents for twine per month to recycle glass, cans, aluminum, and newspapers—less than three minutes daily. It is one of the best possible exercises for children.

### Getting Started

You need only a small space. Storing glass, cans, and newspaper for a month takes only nine square feet in the garage, closet, or a corner of the kitchen or back porch. The only materials required are twine for the newspaper, a can opener, a puncture-type opener, and some stomping (home can crushers can be purchased). Your recycling center usually requires three sturdy boxes: for paper, cans, and glass; bag or box your foil, pie plates, etc. You may prefer to wait for your trip to the recycling center for sorting if you are not as fortunate as Montclair residents whose trash men sort for them. And speaking of foil, remember that it is strong enough for reuse in your own home. Simply clean, if necessary and possible, fold, and store it away for reuse.

## Your Collection Center

If you are out in a rural area you may not need these services, but in most urban and suburban areas you can call your local environmental headquarters or police or sheriff for this information. Often states have recycling hotlines. Some supermarkets redeem aluminum cans. Aluminum companies operate buy-back centers at many landfills. Families who do not have home service like Montclair's often take their recyclables to the local recycling center once a month when they are on other nearby business.

You may have wondered *how* the town or the county handles the recyclable waste. The city of Montclair, New Jersey, sells the materials to a broker who in turn sells them back to industry for processing and re-use. This means a tax saving to you, the local resident through this considerable income.

&#10086; &#10086; &#10086;

After reading this, how do you and I stack up as citizens? How involved are we . . . and our children? How involved *will* we be? It really does not take much. Apart from their involvement with the village of Montclair, Kathie and her boys have for years been collecting aluminum cans for a "little old lady" who is helping some Peace Corps members and missionaries overseas. Since the boys passed the privilege onto us also, Dorothy and I have been picking up cans when we walk up the mountain roads near us and around a nearby golf course. The last load we delivered was close to forty pounds. Let's see now, that would be a savings of about 320 kilowatt-hours or 320 thousand watt-hours which would keep nearly eight thousand forty-watt light bulbs burning for an hour or one such bulb burning night and day for nearly a year. But even better, it has kept some lights burning in hearts overseas, and we won't attempt to measure what it has done for those three little boys!

# SIX

# THEY WHO SERVE: THE TWICE BLESSED

You may have heard our southern California story of the S.O.S. and its *service over self* theme. This kept our children and their neighborhood friends out of trouble when it seemed that youngsters all around them were being dogged by the police or had become pregnant or otherwise were blighting their lives. I was vice president of a university, and, along with our friends, was expected to set an example in the community. For some time we were worried. Our children were busy—Dennis working as a checker at the local supermarket after school and Kathleen helping her mother at home. Yet the pressures were on our family like any others, until we found a formula that was so simple we wondered why we had not thought of it before and why more families or community or church groups didn't use it: Form a secret (or unpretentious) society which did good things for their neighbors or other aged, ill, or needy citizens in town.

They met every Saturday night—when other youngsters were out on the town—to report and to make their altruistic plans and team up to carry them out. They had a great time painting fences, repairing washing machines, weeding gardens, and dozens of other things, usually when their "clients" didn't know it. It was necessary sometimes to notify the police ahead of time that they were going, for example, to take an elderly widower's rocker from his front porch to repair and renew it.

After this book was well on its way, several families wrote us of their service programs. They were so impressive that we realized the element of service deserved a chapter by itself. They made it clear that when your children are motivated by a true spirit of service, whether secret or not, they become much better cooperators in your home management program. They have learned that selflessness is key to sacrificing present pleasures for future benefits.

## Student Service Projects

On my desk at this moment are descriptions of many student projects going on over the world, sponsored by schools, churches, corporations, charitable foundations, and concerned lay groups. For many the pattern calls for children to work and earn the money for their passage; they then go overseas or elsewhere on this continent and build homes, schools, hospitals, and other facilities, or clean up after earthquakes—in China, Japan, Mexico, and San Francisco. We select from these a variety of service experiences typical of the many which have come our way.

Eleven-year-old Donnie Nowell of Sandpoint, Idaho, heard his friends, including family, laymen, pastors and others, calling for prayers for those devastated by the 1989 San Francisco earthquake. He decided that he might help those prayers, so he put an ad in a Sandpoint newspaper, offering to rake leaves to earn money to help the homeless of San Francisco. Linnea Torkelsen writes that "The response was overwhelming. All the fall leaves had just dropped after the first hard frost, and Donnie couldn't keep up with all the requests." When his classmates and sixth-grade teacher discovered his plight, they pitched in and helped him. A week later they sent three hundred dollars to the San Francisco relief effort. The most remarkable result of this creative and thoughtful project was the warming of the children's and their neighbors' hearts.

Amanda Camp, who was once the center of a custody battle, is now giving to others. Her mother reports that Amanda sits "on a regular basis" with an elderly lady who can't afford such services. Now fourteen, she also tutors children who are having study problems, and she helps regularly with feeding and other care for homeless women and children.

The Galen Millers of Ohio work through the Amish and Mennonite churches to raise money for needy in Haiti. From their work with this impoverished country they have learned "what it is like to drive on roads without law and order, and how wonderful it is to be able to walk to the sink and get a drink of water without worrying about malaria." Both parents and children make and sell quilts to earn money for this outreach. In their home town they go as a singing family to cheer guests of nursing homes or other elderly neighbors.

Diane Alme has taken special pains as a state leader in Wisconsin to set down on paper systematic suggestions for families interested in serving, on how to visit, and other ways to show that you care. Her F.I.S.H. program (Families in Schools at Home) which has operated for "many years," involves active, ongoing visitation to area nursing homes which may serve as a model for other kinds of visitation. Their goal is not only to serve those less fortunate than they, but also to provide a high level of socialization for their children and to build in them an instrinsic thoughtfulness and deep compassion. They have enjoyed significant returns on their service to the elderly.

"We've had fun together," she writes, "as we've made seasonal decorations and ornaments with them, and baked goodies, built bird feeders, performed holiday programs, played games, shared special memories, enjoyed sing-a-longs and music puzzles, flown kites, made window gardens, and found friends we otherwise would never have known." Diane also makes a crucially important point which is largely ignored by families today, separated as many are from older relatives and friends: "These [older] people have been through eras most of us just read about in our history books. Their lives are fascinating, and we can learn so much from them."

In 1990, members of F.I.S.H. plan for each family to adopt an elderly resident who may be forgotten by family and friends and also take a day out of the first week of each month and be an encouragement to others. Some are realizing that they have relatives or friends in nursing homes whom they have largely or totally ignored. They have found that responsible youngsters age twelve or older may also become volunteers in transporting wheel chair residents to and from their dining halls, and help with dining room and other duties. F.I.S.H. has set up a telephone central which any person may call if he desires to adopt or volunteer.

## How to Serve Others

"But I haven't the remotest idea," moaned one of our friends recently, "of what to do if I were to visit a hospital or nursing home. Or even a person at home, for that matter." This dilemma is much more common than we realized.

The *first* thing we suggested is to examine your motives for service. If the primary reason is for your own materialistic benefit or to keep up with the Joneses, you may be providing services, but not altruistic service. True service, as we write in this chapter, is an expression on behalf of the welfare of others—a service of selfless love. If you haven't already experienced its rewards in inspiration and uplift, you soon will, as you see others strengthened, inspired, and cheered.

The *second* is to put yourself in those persons' places. Perhaps find out something of their backgrounds, personalities, and accomplishments. Don't dwell on their illnesses, but on positive, upbeat news and views. When we center our minds on others in a positive sense, we forget about ourselves and any selfish "shyness" we may have cultivated.

We join with Diane and others in offering these suggestions about what to do when you make such visits.

- Provide companionship: Just sit and listen and talk, but most often just listen and listen. Don't underestimate the importance of listening. And make sure if any confidences are passed, that you never repeat them.

- Offer to take them to some place of their choosing: shopping, for a walk, perhaps to a park, to a concert, or to church.

- Read to them from something either of you suggest.

- Play games with them—table games, croquet, or others.

- Write a letter or card or wrap a package, and mail them.

- Sing with them or play some of their favorite songs. If you are not a singer or musician, take along some tapes and a recorder.

- Take them some goodies after you have found what they enjoy and can eat, considering their health.

- Make "sunshine boxes" with a variety of little gifts (pens, stationery, toothbrushes, etc.)

- Remember their birthdays or other special days with little notes or cards. If cards, they may appreciate home-made types more.

- Shop for them as necessary.

- Don't overstay your time; it's better to have them wanting you than bored with you.

And we are not speaking only to thoughtfulness for the unfortunate. We could hardly be classified amongst that group, yet usually when Dorothy and I return from one of our many long trips, my sister, Loraine Krieger, known to many of you over the phone for her gentle ways, steps over from her home next door and has some of our favorite dishes and fresh fruit in our refrigerator. Or it may be passing on some significant news from the morning newspaper, or complimenting a particular performance. Thoughtfulness is the oil that lubricates the axles of life and makes the wheels go around smoothly.

## Volunteer Services

Here is a list which many of you have helped put together because you are doing them, and special thanks to Diane.

- Adopt a person
  - Child for a day to clothe or outfit for graduation, etc.
  - Family from church to help with clothes, food, etc.

- Animal training: seeing eye dogs and similar animals

- Anniversaries (Make a list and remember unexpectedly)

- baby-sitting
  - Free
  - Neighbors
  - Church members
  - Family emergencies
  - Parents in trouble

- Baking, etc.
  - Church sales
  - Ill or troubled neighbors
  - School projects

- Birdfeeders
  - Make and stock with seeds and peanut butter, and take to shut-ins to watch

- Candy stripers

- Christmas gifts for neighbors (broadly speaking)
  - Gifts of time or service

- Church
  - Cleaning
  - Office help

- Church organist

- Cleaning houses for needy

- Clipping service for those interested
  - Articles

- Coupons
- Notices
- Quotations

- Cooking
  - Church projects
  - Meals for needy, ill, or to brighten their day

- Flowers
  - Fresh flowers from your garden, even pansies or violets
  - Wild flowers, if you don't have a budget or other supply

- Drives
  - Clothing, for needy
  - Food, for needy
  - Paper and other recycling programs

- Employment (Help aged, handicapped, or ill persons to become involved in some worthy occupation: quilting, painting, etc.)

- Errand running

- Family "meal bags" (non-perishable food items for needy)

- Giving tree to collect items for needy, sort packages into various organizations for pickup and delivery, deliver at most poignant times (Christmas, birthdays, valentines, etc.)

- Health[1]
  - First Aid
  - Health Counsel
  - Treatments

- Help for handicapped

- Holiday activity
  - Arbor Day—seedlings
  - Flag Day/Veterans' Day—cookies, muffins, etc., with flag decor
  - May Day—May Day baskets
  - Valentine's Day—appropriate remembrances
  - Washington's Birthday—something with cherries, etc.

- House cleaning

- Letters with compliments for good mothering, etc.

- Music
  - Instrumental
  - Vocal

- Needy
  - Clothes
  - Food
  - Gifts, special occasions
  - Housing
  - Transportation

- Painting
  - Fences
  - Homes
  - House numbers on curbs, etc.

- Planters to be taken to those who need cheering up
  - Flower seedlings
  - Greenery, particularly to apartment dwellers

- Radio station engineering, etc.
  - Apprentice
  - Volunteer for charitable programs

- Rummage sale for needy

- Sales
  - To earn money for missionaries and needy
  - For altruistic building and stocking project
  - Awana, Pathfinders, Scouts, 4-H, etc.

- Scrap saving (for quilts, patching, crafts, etc.)

- Shopping
  - For elderly and ill
  - For emergencies (hospitalized adults, etc.)

- Sitting
  - House sitting

- Pet sitting

- Snow shoveling

- Surprise bags for children and others leaving on long trips to be opened periodically during journey, to keep them occupied.

- Taking wild flowers to ill or discouraged folks

- Trash removal

- Visitation
    - Convalescent centers
    - Homes
    - Hospitals
    - Nursing homes
    - Prisons

- Walking the feeble/handicapped

- Weeding gardens

- Welcome baskets for new neighbors and those returning home, or sign on the door, or welcome food in their refrigerator.

- Yard work

We repeat, that this list is not exhaustive, nor is it the list of paid services in chapter 11; rather it is for your information and to challenge your imagination. There is something for almost everybody.

# SEVEN

# ORGANIZATION: JUST A LITTLE BIT AT A TIME

A few months ago we again visited Jeanie, a dear and beautiful woman across the Columbia River from our southern Washington home who, with Rich, her faithful husband, owned their comfortable bungalow for many years.[1] They were respectable, church-going citizens, even community leaders concerned for the poor and the sick. But they had a sickness that betrayed their best efforts at helping others: They didn't have to worry about things falling out of their closets; too many of their possessions were stacked outside the doors to get them open more than a few inches. *All* their rooms were filled with random "treasures," most of which had little or no purpose or value. It seems this dear little person seldom could bring herself to eliminate anything. There was no room on their property to build a warehouse, and it is unlikely that it would have been any more organized or orderly if they did. So things which normally would have gone to the Salvation Army, Goodwill, or to the city dump, were dropped wherever there was an inch or foot of space.

Your nostrils would fill with the fragrance issuing from spoiled food pouting in the rear, but both their large freezer and refrigerators were packed so full that you could not retrieve anything from the back without a major evacuation job. The hallways were stacked so full that you had to walk sideways part of the way to the bedrooms and then had no place to sit down except on a partly-loaded bed.

The back porch cried for relief, for it was considerably less organized and orderly than the town dump. The sad state of affairs had long been a focus of family arguments, and Rich bore his cross bravely, until finally, when Jeanie's keepsakes began spilling over into his domain—the back yard and garage—he gave up and joined her garbage club.

I tell you this story, risking your suspicions of exaggeration, but assure you that the picture is understated. This kind of compulsive behavior is well known among psychologists and psychiatrists. I only give you this case for three reasons: First, that no matter how disorganized you may be, there are others who likely have it worse than you; second, what can happen physically and spiritually (or psychologically) if you don't get things in hand; and third, by carelessness with your own personal organization—your health, your figure, and the order in your home—you risk your family unity, a breakup of your marriage, and in this case even your life.

There is no room for sloppiness in clothes, figure, refrigerator, household, garage, yard, and auto. Don't be too proud to bring in a friend who *is* organized and who may have higher standards than you in this respect, but meanwhile we will pass on a few suggestions which have helped us in our home and in administering institutions.

But before we take you too far, let's make it clear that we aren't urging a hasty approach to perfection. This story in fact was one of a perfectionist who became so frustrated with the volume of community and church tasks that even after her children were grown and gone, she couldn't keep up, so she gave up. Such frustration often leads, as with Jeanie, to depression and sometimes to derangement.

Near perfection is the quality we hope our dentist, surgeon, and secretary have in their work, but homemaking with several children under foot may have to accept a little less. More important things, such as the health of your child or the comfort of a guest, must often take precedence over your plans to dust the coffee table, shampoo the rug, or even wash the dishes. We are talking here about approaching a semblance of organization, cleanliness, and order. To settle this will mean a great deal to you in developing self-confidence and self-respect in home management and industries and in passing those qualities on to your children. Perfection may take a little longer.

This responsibility involves consideration of your own mental health—setting aside a time for building your mind with constructive reading, planning, and contemplation. Mothers, particularly, can sometimes be guilty of giving so much time and attention to others that they become drained emotionally. Their own reservoir needs to be filled daily in order to provide the haven of security and peace which the family needs.

Jeanie and Rich were actually a highly skilled couple. Both were professional people. Their income was not large, but it was adequate. Yet their home gave the neighborhood the clear impression of belonging on "the other side of the tracks." Friends and relatives tried gently to counsel. But Jeanie felt hopeless. She feared that if anyone came in to help her clean up "the mess," she would be embarrassed. Her friends had reason to fear for her life. When we visited several days before she died, she confided that her greatest "burden" was about what people would think when they went through her things after she died. And indeed her legacy to her dear ones was the stupendous task of sorting and eliminating the hoardings of the years.

We have found this very concern to be a plague to many parents, particularly mothers, when they have had to face emergency surgery or hospitalization from an automobile accident, and someone else had to come in to care for their young families.

Yet even in Jeanie's extremity, her physical situation wasn't hopeless. The hopelessness was mostly in her mind—the unwillingness to change what had become compulsive behavior, and to lean on others when she couldn't handle the situation herself. She came by her disorder naturally. Her mother was a fair house-keeper, but as is often the case she indulged Jeanie—never making any methodical demands on her. As a parent, her mother had failed in her most important earthly job—training her daughter to be a homemaker.

Nor is this the worst we have seen, only the most recent. Even as we write this, I think of a lady about three miles from our home whose house is so full of her "collections" that she has extended her holdings to her garage and then to a covered porch which runs all around her home. She doesn't seem to realize that she is a spectacle. A psychiatric basket case, you say? Perhaps. But we have seen this happen to several people as they gradually, imperceptibly lost control. We are not sure whether she or Jeanie's type are the more to be pitied, but we hope to help you avoid becoming either.

Nor are we suggesting here that women are the only organiza-tional delinquents. More than one mother has come to us for counsel on how to deal with a junk-minded man. You haven't been far from home if you haven't observed these local residential junkyards. They are generally stocked with old cars, stray tools and implements, old refrigerators, toys, and washing machines, scat-tered helter skelter. Yet whether woman or man, inside or out, each reflects a background of irresponsible rearing or a set of stan-dards which set a low priority on organization and order. Parents who do this are letting their children down, for parental example is their greatest teaching tool, and children deserve better in terms of their own comfort and pride.

Few people in this world are naturally well organized, but it is a skill that can be developed. They might be encouraged to know that psychologically a worse dilemma is to be *over*-organized. Such people suffer constantly and often seriously, stumbling over their own feet as they lose sight of worthy goals in their quest for perfec-tion. They remind us of the ancient Pharisees—not satisfied with a simple washing of their hands before dinner, but they had to re-wash them up to their elbows.

With even a little planning, a pair of young newlyweds shouldn't have any serious problem with housekeeping. They have not accumulated a great many things, or if they have, they often leave their excess stored at their folks' home and their new, little apartment or cottage has a minimal amount of clutter to organize and keep neat. In fact, it's just about perfect. Even if both have jobs out of the home, things stay pretty well under control. But when children arrive, especially the second or third or fourth . . . the trouble begins. That is the time when realistic goals must be set—somewhere between perfectionism and chaos, for people are more important than things.

Most of our disorganized friends seem to have the idea that they have to make the change all at once. Forget it! Only take as much as you can chew and chew it thoroughly. But not so thoroughly that you spend all the time you have to spend on one part of the house and let the rest of the house suffer for weeks or months.

Dr. James Dobson tells of an incident in their family before they had any children when both he and his wife, Shirley, were new teachers. Because of the demands of their jobs, they were short of housekeeping time and things had gotten ahead of them. He tells that when he returned from a required meeting one evening, Shirley had gotten involved with cleaning the stove, taking it apart and cleaning it meticulously during a total of three hours. In the process she was thrown behind in a number of other household areas. Ever since, they have humorously identified any of their compulsive behavior which unreasonably interferes with their real needs as a "stove job."

In hindsight, common sense says that if you have three hours or only thirty minutes, budget your time according to your priorities. This is the place where divide and conquer does the trick. If cleaning the stove was tops on her list, it may be that Shirley should have given it a total of ten minutes—even using a kitchen timer as a gentle discipliner. A timer is a great organizational tool! Or if time allowed, she could have taken out the drip pans to soak in hot, soapy water while she wiped off the rest and then washed them before returning them to the stove, perhaps for a total of twenty to thirty minutes. With few exceptions in homemaking, it is better to have everything less than perfect than nothing done at all. Moderation is one of wisdom's crown jewels.

Get help from your family where you can. But don't put it off, for it is not going to be any better tomorrow or next month or next year. The older you get, the less likely you are to get it all together. Your friends and family make larger and larger demands, your program only gets busier, and your "junk" or dirt keeps piling up.

Though the middle of the road is not always a safe place to be, somewhere between perfectionism and procrastination is the goal to be reached. Budget your time as you should budget your money, making it stretch as far as you can without stressing you to the breaking point. With whatever time you have, divide it up between needs. Make use of bits of time. We think of one mother who had a lot of phone planning to do in connection with her church work. She had a very long cord on her telephone in the kitchen and cradled the phone on her neck while she did her kitchen chores. The cordless phone is convenient for this too, or a head set much like a telephone operator's with no cord; think of all the jobs that could be done during average phoning time! And she learned to really use her calls and calling time.

Now let's talk about how to start, how to take it a little bit at a time. Yet this doesn't mean that you don't have a long range plan. After you set your goals, you can get on with the details—which we will introduce later. You might be astonished at the many basics that most people ignore as if they were not essential to organization and order. Let's start with a list of *priorities* which could be entitled "Organization and Order in My Life" and set it up something like this:

- *Order in my heart.* Whom do I love most, myself or others?

- *Order in my body.* Do I have my appetite, exercise, rest, and physique under reasonable control?

- *Order in my family.* Do I have the respect of my spouse and my children?

- *Order in my house.* Is my house reasonably well organized and my time allotted for optimum efficiency?

## Order in My Heart

The history of man clearly demonstrates that it is in our nature that we human beings look to a being higher than ourselves. Reaching out and upward, I have found, is much more effective than trying to pull myself up by my own bootstraps.

You need to set aside time for pulling things together and for building your mind with constructive reading, planning, prayer, and contemplation. So, find yourself an appropriate little nook or nooks to provide for your own equilibrium, including a desk, even an improvised one, with materials for handling bills, correspondence, daily planning, etc. When you open the daily mail, sit by a waste basket and try to handle each item only once, sometimes writing an answer on the margin or bottom of a letter and returning it promptly.

Mothers, particularly, are sometimes guilty of giving so much time and attention to others that they become drained emotionally. Their own reservoir needs to be periodically refilled with an appropriate balance of solitude, rest, recreation, and study in order to provide the haven of security and peace which the family needs.

Annapolis, Maryland's Loris Nebbia was one frustrated mother who, we found out later, wanted to write a book, but didn't have enough quiet hours in the day and night. Although she had chosen to teach her children at home, her story is one that could come from any mother. She was the mother of four children: Eric, ten; Joseph, eight; Valerie Jeanne, five; and Karl, three. She was greatly encouraged by the obedient, loving family involvement of Eric and Joseph. As she wrote to Dorothy in quest of counsel, she said they were "busy making lunch for the little ones." Valerie Jeanne "is naturally sweet and joyful." But Karl was something else: Sometimes "He can be an absolute lamb, but he is often very loud and demanding and willful." She thought a principal reason might be "the noise and activity level in the house." And apparently she felt either unorganized or disorganized, afraid that she was "doing nothing well. The house is not as it should be." And she was conscience-stricken because she was not more "involved with church activities."

Her desperation was expressed in the final words of her letter of September 16, 1988:

It's just that I feel that I am doing nothing well. . . . I just don't think that I can cope any longer with feeling so stretched, and such a failure. . . .

As September drew near this summer, I was once again confronted by the usual comments where I went. "I'll bet you're glad all those kids will be back in school in a couple of days!" they all say to me. I used to say, "No!" emphatically. This year I just smiled. My children weren't going back to school, but I sure wished they were! With all my heart I wished that all four of them were going somewhere to school. I feel awful about these feelings that I have. I have always tried to keep such feelings out of my heart. It is my opinion that such feelings are inappropriate. Mothers shouldn't feel that way! But they do, and I do too, as sorry as I am to have to admit it. Even though every mother in the nation is ecstatic when her children go back to school, I was determined that I would not be. "Mine stay home, I am not anxious to get rid of my children," I'd say to myself. But this year, I couldn't say it and be truthful. What is wrong with me that I have gotten to dislike home schooling as much as I have? If I dislike it so much, why don't I just quit? I don't feel like I can quit, either. I feel as if I must home school because that is the best thing for my children. Is there any way you can help? . . . Thanks for listening and for all the help you and your husband have been over the years.

Like Loris's moving but direct report, so was Dorothy's explicit answer—good for any mother, home teacher or not—and as it turns out, with immense meaning for any mother or father who is unorganized or burning out. After apologizing for her delayed answer—because of an extended itinerary for seminars in Australia and New Zealand, Dorothy wrote exactly three months later. Here are excerpts; other counsel will emerge in the exchange below.

[Yes], I have an answer for you. Our new book, *Home School Burn-out,* was written just for mothers [and fathers] like you. My only regret is that I did not tell you about it sooner. Yet the books only came from the publisher two weeks ago.

Until you send for it, just let me make a few suggestions. Be a little easier on yourself—get more rest, worry less about your children's education (they're already excelling) and just enjoy them. My guess is that you are trying too hard to have "school at home." Let your big boys do more things that they want to do, as long as it is constructive—even if it's reading the encyclopedia instead of the history book!

How early do you get to bed? The hours before midnight are worth twice as much as the hours after midnight for quality sleep. Perhaps you are *giving* too much of yourself. Mothers have quite a tendency to do that, I know. Do you have a whole household "quiet time" for about an hour after lunch every day? You need this much solitude for your peace of mind. Maybe you're too much of a perfectionist. My confession on that is in the book.

How about starting to write down, yes, write down, some of your blessings? Actually, you did write down many, in your letter to me. Your boys scored high academically and display beautiful character traits. Your daughter has a sweet temperament, naturally sweet and joyful. And how wonderful to have a cooperative, supportive husband. Is there any part of his business in which he could involve the older boys? Or could he get them started in some kind of home industry? And perhaps spend more time with them on the weekends, if not through the week? That would give you more time with your little ones and perhaps more time for yourself.

P.S. It just occurs to me that a little more consistent discipline to keep the "noise and activity level in the house" under control might be one of your answers. Temporary isolation for the older ones and perhaps a few minutes sitting on a chair for the three-year-old. They need to learn self-restraint in this.

Less than a month later Loris's letter lit up our mailbox, glowing like the dawn of a clear morning. We had not dared to expect so remarkable a change in so short a time. "I was so grateful," she wrote, "to receive your letter."

One of the things that is hardest for me is to accept the fact that I, too, have needs and capacities. My need for solitude is real, and important. . . .

I was frustrated about one thing that I may not have expressed in my letter to you. I am trying to write a book. I did not feel that I could ask my family for time to do this. But when I expressed my feelings, they proved to be more generous than I had assumed and have been very supportive.

My husband and I went through your book, *Homebuilt Discipline* for suggestions . . . and decided to try to get to bed early and rise earlier. It has made a tremendous difference for us. It gives me quiet time, without interruption [in the early morning] to express myself in writing, and he enjoys studying. Of course, if he hadn't agreed to the earlier bedtime, it would have been more difficult for me to do, so I am grateful. . . .

I was trying to "entertain" or keep the big boys busy all the time. You helped me to see that was unnecessary. . . . Joey said to me today, "Thanks for letting us stay home from school. Most kids don't get even one year with their parents."

I appreciated your idea of a quiet hour right after lunch. The boys accepted the idea as if it were the most natural thing in the world, and so I have been retreating to my room for an hour, while they work quietly and are not permitted to speak to each other. The mandate for silence cuts down on brotherly play, and they have been getting a lot done. I return in an hour feeling like an entirely different person.

I've also tried the idea of giving my three-year-old exercise in self-restraint by requiring him to sit quietly in a chair for a few minutes. That was a great idea. Even the words that you wrote—"They need to learn self-restraint in this," were enlightening, because it made me think about the noise problem as a *family* problem, not *my* problem. . . .

P.S. My husband thanks you for the letter, too. He has been working hard on a project at work and was surprised with the award of "comp" time (compensation). He decided to come home early on Wednesday afternoon and take over for the day so I can have some time. This week they did a chemistry experiment and a neighbor child came over to join us!

Loris found that in some ways, we do not expect enough from our children. When you expect more in self-control, consideration of others, and in manual work, you will activate perhaps the most efficient and effective tools of discipline—even when they are little rebels.

## Order in My Body

If I don't have my body—and my personal lifestyle—under reasonable control, my self-respect will inevitably go out the window. I will begin to rationalize, to blame, to suffer, and to force others to suffer with me—or to ignore or leave me. Such is not a comfortable nest in which to incubate and hatch the eggs of organization and order. There is no substitute for self-control. I may develop my semblance of organization and order, but it will be an uphill battle if I don't start with my own body, my own appetite, and set an example for my family.

Time invested in a balanced health program for both you and your family is time well spent and no part can safely be neglected. The health record of our nation, the most affluent nation on earth, may also be the most shameful on earth in sheer indulgence and waste; partly, in fact, because of American ability to afford rich and fast foods rather than be satisfied with simple, natural things which the poverty of "underdeveloped" countries demands, but which brings them better health. Japan and Korea in their new prosperity are now following our decadent practice of insisting that wants become needs.

However, recent studies of lifestyles in China confirm our long-held conclusion that a simple low-fat, high-fiber diet derived from plant foods is the one that not only improves longevity but also enhances the quality of life. Some of our friends shrug this one off, but the evidence is becoming so overwhelming that we think sooner or later you will see the wisdom. Natural foods, as nearly as possible the way they grow, make food preparation much less time-consuming and more nutritious for your family.

Common problems which wear mothers out are children's illnesses and discipline. These can be minimized by some very simple methods. After reading our book *Home Made Health,* one mother wrote, "I used to think naps and regular bedtimes were old-fashioned. No one ever told me children needed them. I wondered why my two-year-old was always so sick. Just by making sleeping and eating habit changes, we cut our discipline problems in half!"

Some may think the following statement extreme and out of place in this book, but we'll gladly take our chances on this, considering the evidence: A truly informed and well-managed home will not be spending much money on soft drinks and sugared and fatty items for its children, nor preferably even the parents. Not only are these unnecessary for sustaining life, and costly in money, but they almost invariably and eventually incur heavy losses—in mental and physical health and in time. Here again we see that golden thread and management principle that runs through this book: The sacrifice of present pleasures for future benefits.

According to doctors, the most common complaint they hear from women is fatigue, especially if they have young children. Some people seem to accept the idea that during the first year or two of any child's life, mother needs to be disturbed several times each night. Though her mother love would never drive her to feel resentful, she seldom gets a full night's rest, and as some have described it, is often a walking zombie during the day.

Because mothers need to be at the their best to handle their homemaking cares, it is of urgent importance that they get a full uninterrupted night's rest. This is possible, except, of course, in case of the illness of any member of the family. For more information on how to train babies to sleep through the night, see the author's book, *Homebuilt Discipline,* and its new study guide.[2]

Budgeting time for exercise also will more than repay you in energy and peace of mind. Brand-new, encouraging information has come via the results of the most comprehensive fitness study ever conducted—of 13,344 men and women over fifteen years—showing that a little exercise goes a long way. Only thirty minutes of brisk walking a day for five days a week is needed to fend off deadly illness. The enormous contrast is between those who don't exercise at all and those who exercise moderately. For your comfort, Steven N. Blair who directed the study at Dr. Kenneth H. Cooper's Institute for Aerobics Research in Dallas said, "Brisk leaf-raking, vigorous vacuuming, sports—it doesn't matter." [3]

## Order in My Family

We talk fully and conclusively about developmental needs of children, and parent-child and parent-school relationships in such research- and experience-based books as *Better Late Than Early, Home Grown Kids, Homebuilt Discipline, Home Made Health,* and *Home School Burnout.* These include powerful research evidence demonstrating that children who are not institutionalized early generally are significantly higher achievers, better behaved, and more positively socialized. There is no substitute for family values in building a foundation for family order and organization. Obviously, you will do better in a family business if you get along among yourselves and demonstrate mutual confidence and dedication to mutual goals.

## Order in My House

Here and in the next two sections we get down to points on order and organization. At the outset let's agree that no two houses are exactly alike. With one the size is too large with too much upkeep; another is too small and without storage room. One houses a family whose four children are under age six, while another covers the perplexity of three willful children entering their teens. One is governed by parents whose enthusiasm overbounds their common sense, and another harbors a mother and dad who are afraid of their own shadows. So we will deal more in larger principles and applications common to all.

Here order in my house demands that we take up these common organization and order trouble spots one at a time: the kitchen, the closets, the garage, the car, and the yard. And we suggest that you choose, study, and organize them one at a time, depending, of course, on your family situation. Cheered with your success and without an overload, you will go on with greater confidence to the other areas. And remember what we said about Jeanie: in both the planning and implementation, don't be too proud to counsel with friends who excel in your areas of need.

If you are a mother with four children under age six, you are in what might be called a "holding operation." Yet many mothers are surprised when we show them how much each child can do in helping to *keep* things neat. Our eighteen-month-old grandson learned well that he could not take more than two books out of the book shelf at a time and that they must be returned before he could start any other activity or get more books. The same rule applied to toys or groups of toys, such as blocks. A plastic laundry basket held his toys in the family room. We discovered also that at that age he could unload the dishwasher and help set the table. Our daughter, Kathleen, arranged to use an undercounter shelf for the dishes instead of a high cupboard.

A six-year-old, of course, can be quite efficient at cleaning the bathroom wash bowl and tub, washing dishes, doing errands in the house, sweeping porches and walks, and many other jobs if they are taught how. If in your desperation or to avoid it, you can conquer your perfectionism and train your children—not just send them off to do a job—you will reap big dividends for yourself and build your child's self-concept, especially if you help him feel he is on the family team and show your appreciation for the jobs he does.

## The Kitchen and the Bathroom

These should be the cleanest rooms in the house, because the health of the family largely depends on cleanliness and sanitation. First, let's talk about ways to avoid unnecessary cleaning. If you follow this plan, you will seldom have a major cleaning job. It takes much less time to keep things clean than it does to allow things to build up to a giant project.

Unless you have a self-cleaning oven and non-stick drip pans which wash like teflon, put a large sheet of aluminum foil on the bottom of the oven, being careful not to let it touch the element, and also cover your drip pans with foil. Then, of course, take special care and perhaps use a timer to help you avoid having pans boil over. Wipe up spills immediately. Such management will seldom require an extended time for super-cleaning.

The same type of preventive plan will keep the refrigerator in good shape with very few major cleaning jobs. Plan to use leftovers promptly to save spoilage and keep your refrigerator from being cluttered. Even little dabs are often someone's favorite and if they are not, try to incorporate them into a casserole or other recipe. Let this be an ongoing fun project to challenge your creativity. If you shop for fresh produce once a week, hopefully on the day your market gets in their new supply, rinse or wipe out the vegetable drawer and possibly a shelf or two before you fill them up again. Wipe up spills when they happen, and don't let problems accumulate.

Train everyone in the family who is old enough to pick up his dishes at the end of a meal and carry them to the sink. Most should also rinse and add them to separate stacks or piles of bowls, plates, and utensils no matter who is going to wash them.

If drawer and cupboard space is limited, hang pans and also utensils, if you can, to save counter space. Otherwise, use a heavy crock or other appropriate container on the counter or on the stove to hold utensils vertically.

Keep cleaning supplies handy in both kitchen and bathroom(s) so that you can swish out the bathroom washbowl, or even clean the whole bathroom, when you are in there supervising baby's pre-bath playtime. Have a mesh bag for baby's bath toys which he can learn to fill when playtime is over.

I am well acquainted with a lady who is compulsive about washing clothes, and she has made her whole family so. Just because most everything is washable these days and clothes which require dry cleaning are less common does not mean that everything must be washed every time it is worn. Yet this is the habit in this family and that includes kitchen and bathroom towels. She not only wears out washing machines but also clothes, and what a waste of time! The watch word again is moderation!

To dry the body after a daily shower or bath should not require a clean towel every time. Depending on the drying time of your weather, a set of towels can be allotted to each family member at reasonable intervals which they are to keep neatly hung on individual racks at heights to accommodate even the little ones.

Even the drawers, cupboards, floor, and woodwork can profit from this preventive plan. BUT if things have gotten out of hand, then use that kitchen timer and budget your time with a little cleaning at a time in order of priority. Do as those addicted to tobacco or drugs are told to do: Make a firm determination to "choose to clear up your problems—a little bit at a time." Some of us are accumulators. Beware of its becoming addictive. If you have had to move often and do your own packing, you have probably learned one solution—develop buyer-resistance, especially to "bargains," even to some bargains at garage sales which you do not really need. The other is to eliminate things you never use, even many of the things you hope to use someday, but realistically, never will. Give away, throw away, or have a garage sale, perhaps with another family, so you won't have so much clutter to contend with. Remember, one man's trash is another man's treasure.

## The Closets

So many have written or asked in seminars for suggestions, usually protesting that they just don't have enough drawers, hangers, and shelves, assuming, of course, that they have eliminated the "never used" items. When we didn't have enough of these (or other cubby holes), we got some strong cardboard boxes from the local supermarkets and lined them (optional) with plastic sheeting or similar material, plainly marking them with each youngster's name or logo (which each child can invent for himself and put on with a large crayon or other marker). Some of these can be stored under their beds—one or two each for clothes, toys, and miscellany.

You will eliminate a lot of unhappiness all the way around if you have a law of the Medes and Persians that says, "All clothes and toys will be put away properly on penalty of being confiscated" with payment of money or special jobs to redeem them—or other plan which you make clear. It will help a great deal if you make it a game. But this is a matter of testing your consistency if you hope to make it work. And it just might be fair if you, too, are under the same constraints. This brings parental example to the testing point. Children will gladly check you out on this—and respect you for it.

We made slight modifications in our closets which we now find are quite common. Except for dresses and overcoats, full-length hanging space in a closet is normally a waste. The average closet can easily accommodate two rods, so that you have blouses, shirts, jackets and trousers hanging two high. Now take your children into the closet with you, if you can get in, and show them how to hang their pants together, shirts together, etc. Dad will want to hang suits or trade uniforms or other things together, white shirts by themselves, etc. Sweaters and shirts can be either hung or placed on a shelf or in boxes or drawers. And be sure to have plenty of hangers around, even wire hangers, so that no one has an excuse to leave his clothes lying around.

No shoes should ever go into the closet until they are ready for wearing the next time. If they are dusty or muddy, they should be left on the back porch until they are cleaned or polished. In Japan, you leave them in the *genkan* or inner front porch. Children can be trained to be expert in shoe-shining responsibilities as young as age seven or eight. They might well be paid for this service, and as we mention in our industry list, when they become genuinely skillful, they may develop shoe shining into a cottage industry. In any event, why not delegate shoe care to a certain child, changing off to others as you think wise.

If you still don't have enough closet room, you might try sentencing out of season clothes to restriction on a clothing rod in the attic or basement where they will be covered with an old bed spread, sheet, or other cover. This also gives you an opportunity to eliminate those you no longer need—remembering Goodwill, Salvation Army, your church rummage sale, or even your own garage sale or personal charity.

## The Garage

A person doesn't have to be a Ph.D. to know when a garage is dirty and disheveled. Yet it is astonishing how many families advertise their personal and family standards by an open garage door. In most garages this problem can be simply and quickly remedied in a variety of ways, depending on your problem: For rakes, shovels and similar tools, nail a two-by-four solidly to the garage wall at a six- to eight-foot height and pound in sixteen- to twenty-penny nails as hooks, or if your garage is rough, unlined inside, nail short two-by-fours on either side of a stud, extending out.

Bicycles can be easily hung by their wheels, using cushioned hooks which you can screw into ceiling joists. Any rolling equipment—lawn mowers, wheelbarrows—look much better if they are lined up pointing in the same direction. And small items like paints, fertilizer solutions, and soaps enjoy reclining on neat, inexpensive shelves bracketed to your garage wall. Strong brackets are available at hardware or discount stores and are simple to install. Then top this off with a large trash container. Finally, bringing your whole family into your plan will make it much more effective.

## The Car

Have you looked at the floor of your car lately? If it is neat and clean, you are a rare bird, or you may have a chauffeur or special attendant (liked a well-trained daughter or son). At least three or four out of five autos in which we ride these days or which visit our office are unhappy about the way their owners ignore their insides, and usually their faces as well. There is seldom any real excuse for such inhumane treatment of the inside of a helpless car, particularly if you have a child around who is six or older. And with reasonable training and help from an adult, a youngster of eight to ten can also do a creditable job on the car's outside—washing its "face." For a youngster of that age, it's great to work with dad or mother. The cleanliness of your car, outside and in, is a remarkably accurate measure of your personal standards.

## The Yard

Yards are so variable that we won't attempt much counsel here. Some are large, some small; some fenced, some open; some lawned, some concrete; some trim, some scrubby. The first thing, in any event, whether your lot is acreage or the size of a postage stamp, is to get rid of clutter and litter. This may mean anything from a stray tumbleweed, beer can, piece of paper, or cardboard box to old pipe or dead automobiles. But get rid of them, front and back! After that, get whatever advice you can find for a lawn or garden or flowers or other improvement within the limits of your pocket book. Having your front door clean and your house reasonably well painted is a plus.

## Yourself

Here we find ideas from organizational expert Pat Burris, whose ideas are simple and direct.[4] They are remarkably like those Dorothy wrote in our book, *Home School Burnout,* and which I can testify she practices consistently in all areas of her life. Although most of these pieces are written in behalf of women, they more often than not offer both principles and methods for men as well. Author Shellee Nunley, by way of introducing Pat, throws out this challenge:

> 'Fess up. Do you own:
> - A kitchen drawer that's a black hole, sucking up a ridiculous assortment—clothespins, nails, a refrigerator warranty, a 1987 sweepstakes entry form, and birth certificate?
> - A garment you've been meaning to take to the cleaners for at least a month?
> - No proof of having filed last year's tax return—only a vague recollection?
> - If you can't relate to any of these, go read the comics. Your life is in order, and you deserve to trifle.

In addition to the long phone cord idea, Pat Burris offers these organizational minima which we suggest that you take one at a time as your first gesture in gaining control:

*Streamline your home.* Get rid of clutter. She says, "It makes us feel out of sync, disoriented, and anxious." (Our friends, Jeanie and Rich, were pathetic in this respect.) Pat then observes that "space is calming and helps you feel in control." Next, organize so that you keep similar items together, and in logical spots—spices near the stove, breakfast cereals above the refrigerator where the rising heat tends to keep them dry, cups and glasses convenient to your drinking patterns. In one kitchen drawer you can place a cardboard box to hold your mixes and small package items.

*Know your energy cycle.* If, as should be normal, you have more energy in the morning, use that time to do your most demanding chores, particularly those which require brain power. Your body battery has hopefully been recharged overnight, so your mind performs much more efficiently early in the day than after supper at night, unless you have had a good mid-day nap (which we recommend). Pat Burris does most of her writing and other creative work in the morning, a practice which we also recommend to students, particularly those who must work while they go to school. Save your simple manual work—ironing, button-sewing, and casual errands—for afternoon.

You can virtually double your time by going to bed early at night, for the time before midnight is worth two to three times that after midnight for sound rest. And the time before breakfast in the morning—while the electrical current to the brain is strong and the blood is not yet surrendered to your stomach to digest your food—is worth three to five times that after supper at night when the body is tired, the electrical current running down, and the blood surrendered to the abdomen.

*Have an errand box.* Keep this box near the door that goes out to the car. Here you will keep items to be dry-cleaned, coupons for the store, library books to be returned, packages to be mailed. Set up safeguards for priority items or things easy to forget by writing yourself notes and taping them in obvious places. For example, if you should phone someone while phone rates are cheapest, attach your note to the phone.

*Set up a simple filing system.* Here again you can use a shoe box or other cardboard container for bills to pay, letters to answer, tasks to complete, errands you have placed on hold, menu plans, and other activities.

*Take time to plan.* Pat Burris insists that "If you fail to plan, you plan to fail." We agree. Plan at the beginning of each week, on Saturday or Sunday night, and every night when the children are settled. Dorothy has long had a system which complements this: Have a daily slip of paper for meal planning and use of leftovers. She has another for tasks to do or errands to run today or in the near future—in order of priority—and finally, a shopping list. She goes over them at the end of the day, checks off the things she has done, and makes out new lists where necessary. This takes less than five minutes, and she moves with confidence through her day. It will also help you to make an orderly list for your shopping day so that your itinerary does not require you to unnecessarily retrace your steps.

*Have a coded calendar.* This is a calendar with large squares for each day. Buy one or make one; your youngsters will like to help you. Assign a certain color of pencil to each family member who is old enough to handle this. Let them mark their activities. At a glance you will be able to see how to avoid conflict and make the most of appointments.

*Learn to use "dead" time.* When you are waiting at the shoe shop, beauty shop, car wash, or doctor's office, take important reading or other projects with you.

## Pack Rats

Before we leave you and "organization," we pass on the promised ideas of how to deal with the kind of compulsive behavior we saw in Jeanie, which is shared in a lesser degree by all too many of us and which often becomes a major barrier to personal organization. Psychologist L. W. Warren would have called her a "pack rat" [PR], and insist that she was convinced that all the materials she hoarded were "valuable and have potential."[5] Many of us are aware that we already have those PR tattoos all over us; others, more tragically, don't know. The first thing, says Warren's colleague, J. Ostrom, is to "fix it."

Are you (or a member of your family) really a pack rat, a compulsive shopper, gatherer, obtainer—and a candidate for hopelessness in personal and home organization? How do you know? Another psychologist, Perry Buffington, quotes from Warren and Ostrom's new book, *Pack It Away,* (scheduled for publication in 1991), which helps you identify the symptoms of the troubled pack rat.[6] How do you feel about others visiting you? Do you fear being found out or losing control of your habit?

The compulsive hoarder seems much like the compulsive eater. All who successfully fight the battle of the dietary bulge learn that you have to get down to your weight goal and then practice a lifestyle that keeps you there. They call this "weight loss" and "maintenance." Similarly, professors Warren and Ostrom label their remedy "cut back skills and structure." Once the pack rat knows he has a problem, he must study its nature, its complexity, realizing that this kind of behavior is not simple to change. Wise pack rats will seek the counsel and cooperation of their families or others in whom they trust. Some have suspected such compulsive behavior to be akin to the kleptomaniac who impulsively takes things from stores or elsewhere without any need for them and without paying.

First, say Warren and Ostrom, they must determine "to bring less into their environment." This may mean canceling subscriptions, staying away from tempting places such as flea markets and discount stores, wrecking yards, or old book stores.

Second, they must learn to sort and dispose. Their decisions will be strengthened if they make a list of worthy or needy individuals, institutions, or charities. They will have to face up to the fact that some items may have to go to junk dealers or to the town dump. In Washougal, Washington, we bought a piece of property which had been an eyesore for decades, just to clean it up and eventually resell it. The owners had twenty-three old refrigerators, stoves, washers, and dryers lounging around those acres, not to mention thirteen old rusted cars. They had no idea of organization or cleanliness or order. Junk dealers and car buffs helped us out in quick order.

Third, develop structure or maintenance skills like keeping your desk clean, quickly eliminating unneeded mail, and cleaning house. With the development of this last set of habits, the pack rat, says Warren, begins to think more like a tosser—people who throw away everything (although we don't suggest that you go to this extreme).

Bruce and Kathleen Kordenbrock have established a rule this year for their three boys. Their rooms couch a surplus of toys—little cars, big cars; little airplanes, big airplanes; blocks, puzzles, trikes, and bikes. You name it, they have it—given them by friends, relatives, and by parents who now realize that they may have been a bit indulgent at times. So the rule is that the toy collection must be thoughtfully and substantially reduced before next Christmas or there will be no Christmas presents. This means decisions, decisions, decisions: which toys to let go, who to take them or ship them to, when to do it—heavy decisions for three-, seven-, and ten-year-olds, but a worthy exercise in thoughtfulness, order, and generosity in any family.

Finally, if you are afraid that you will never be organized, write down on a sheet of paper each item in this chapter that applies to you, and then set out to do one thing at a time: Check off the first, then go on to the second, until you have things well in hand. *Keep it simple.* You can become more sophisticated about your organization later. If you have a place for everything and everything in its place, even if it is only a cardboard box for umbrellas on the back porch or for toys in the corner of the kids' room, you are started on an organizational pattern, and you are a more confident person than you have ever been.

# PART TWO

---

# HOME INDUSTRIES

# EIGHT

# THE MIRACLE OF WORK: HOW HANDS BUILD THE HEAD AND THE HEART

A most simple but poignant story on the work ethic came to us recently from Professor H. L. Goodwin, Jr. when we were discussing home industries during an Austin, Texas, seminar. I asked him to put his story down briefly on paper to show how children who learn to work usually do better than average in business and the professions. Note the ages at which he, a boy, mastered various tasks, the long-term effects of his work experiences, and the parts his parents and their expectations played in his own little drama. Note what happens when you grant a child authority commensurate with the responsibility he accepts:

> I grew up on a farm in northeast Oklahoma. When I was eight, my dad gave me a heifer and told me when she calved I got to keep any heifers, and he got all bull calves. By the time I was twelve, I had my own checkbook, bought and sold any additional cattle, and dealt with all feed and other expenditures. When I was eighteen, I received a State Farmer Award from Future Farm-

ers of America, graduated valedictorian with a 4.0 from my class of 238 and scored a composite 30 on the A.C.T. [in large part from this work].

My cattle and then swine operations paid my way through college and M.S. and Ph.D. programs at Oklahoma State University. Currently I am a tenured Associate Professor of Agricultural Economics at Texas A. and M. University. We will home school all our children and are currently in the process of buying a farm so our children can also gain the benefits I learned from hard work, responsibility, and creativity of management on the farm. I assume any business would accomplish the same things.

My parents taught me at an early age to work, save, and give (I mowed yards for 25 cents each at age 6). John Wesley's philosophy, "Work all you can, save all you can, and give all you can," certainly seems appropriate to me!

By the way, I never had a curfew, but I never violated my parents' trust in me. Besides, if I stayed out too late, I still had farm chores which began at 6:00 A.M. Pretty good incentive structure, don't you think?

The remarkable thing about the work experience is what we call its synergic effect—by combining his hand and his head, Dr. Goodwin accomplished far more in a given time than he would if he had spent all his time on either his head or his hands alone. The experience brought him excellence, not only in academic and manual skills, but also in his mental and physical health and his moral or spiritual values—valuing his time and his responsibility to others.

Another example of this work ethic is Guillermo Garcia, an Indio, California Mexican. It is not only because of his Mexican ancestry that we tell a little of his story, but also to show how anybody with some ambition and willingness to work can do very well.

As we write this, Guillermo has just done a masterful job on the electrical system of our home. I emphasize his qualifications as a master electrician, for he came in and quickly set in order a seriously malfunctioning electrical system which, as the result of another electrician's carelessness, made our home a fire hazard. He is an electrical contractor with the highest standards and is in demand in California's Coachella Valley.

Guillermo has worked and saved since before he was twelve. When he was fifteen, he got a job in an Indio fruit and vegetable packing shed where he worked from the time school dismissed at 3 P.M. until two o'clock the next morning. While we would not recommend such a strenuous program for anyone, this boy did it on his own. Before he was sixteen, he made a down payment on his first house and made payments from the rent he received for it. When he got out of high school (with good grades) he worked at first for very low pay as an apprentice electrician and continued until he received his license as a master and contractor.

Yet all was not rosy. In 1983 there was a sharp downturn in construction in the desert, and electrical jobs were scarce. So Guillermo pocketed his pride and went into the tomato and asparagus fields to earn his living with a laborer's hands and heart. Now in his early thirties, he has paid for his home, car, and truck, and has twenty-five thousand dollars in the bank. And at home his wife cares for his three sons—ten, eight, and six—except when they are with him on the job.

Dorothy and I recently met Caroline Frommhold on a flight from Austin, Texas, to Salt Lake City. Caroline was on her way to Alaska to coordinate a conference—an exciting assignment for a young lady in her early twenties. We asked her how she became an "Institute Coordinator" for a major conference planning company. Her answer was simple enough:

> I worked my way through high school; had a part time job most of those years. Then in my senior year, a friend of mine in church told me about management internships. Lots of companies have them. I applied, and my typing and other things were good enough for them to put me on for a part-time job. That led to another job the next semester, and my boss there kept me on all the way through college. When I found that there was a choice to work in the office or to travel for the company, I asked to travel since I was still single, and here I am.

There are no two persons who enjoy precisely the same route to a good job. But in all cases there must be an appreciation of the

importance of doing the job well, and of being willing to work—
instead of looking for the easy way out.

## The Lessons of Work-Study Programs

Tucked away in the hills of Tennessee is a small high school that
just might be a lighthouse to storm-whipped American schools and
homes. With tools in one hand and books in the other—literally—
the teachers lead their students through a day divided about
equally between manual work and study. And sensing the closeness
of values school life should have with family life, their parents send
their children there for that very reason. Their children have been
working at home, and they don't want them to lose that ethic as
they begin life away from the family.

This may seem like the lifestyles of George Washington, Abraham Lincoln, Thomas Edison, or George Carver, but that's not
really so bad. Performance of working students on standardized
tests both here and abroad significantly excels the non-working
pupil. And serious behavior problems in such schools and homes
are virtually non-existent. The hundreds of thousands of students
in California high schools' Regional Occupational Programs
(ROPs) testify to it. The same is true of colleges from coast to
coast like Warren Wilson in North Carolina, Blackburn in Illinois,
School of the Ozarks in Missouri, and Weimar in California. It is
even true of Deep Springs, the tiny California college with a Nevada post office address, whose students average twenty hours or
more manual work weekly and which routinely sends its students
on to Cornell, Berkeley, Yale, Harvard, Chicago, Stanford, and
Swarthmore.

And the universities are not without their sparkling models. In
the mid-sixties, when I was with the U.S. Office of Education, we
were asked to evaluate Boston's Northeastern University for a possible graduate chemistry/physics facility grant. The first reaction of
most of our USOE staff was not positive. Some grant committee
members didn't consider Northeastern a leading scientific institution worthy of its distinguished neighbors—Harvard, MIT, Tufts,

and others. They reasoned that the nine or ten thousand students then on work/study programs would offer no special sanctuary of scholarship, spending as they did alternating semesters in classes and at work.

This worried me, for as president of work/study colleges in Japan, the Philippines, and Texas, I had found the opposite to be true. And upon closer look, Northeastern was not an exception: Not only did the university have a reputable faculty, but the work/study program brought in what amounted to more than thirty million dollars annually in endowment income from more than twenty-three hundred participating corporations, some of them highly-scientific operations. The committee discovered that Northeastern had one of America's best employment records for its graduates. And it had a broader than average gift base, for it seems that donors are often partial to workers. Northeastern got the grant.

Calloused hands effectively hone receptive minds, and somehow they warm and enlarge hearts. Where most or all of the teachers work *with* the students as at Warren Wilson and Weimar and at tiny Deep Springs, the evidence is even clearer. Morale is much higher when teacher and student work shoulder to shoulder. And in the home this adult-child team-up reaches its zenith. So also is the adult influence seen in its most powerful form when parents work with their children at home. There is also in the work ethic some remarkable synergic effect that brings much higher production proportionately, and infinitely deeper self-respect when teacher and student join in exploring the union of head, hand, and heart than either teacher or student can produce alone. When the youngsters can see something practical and profitable produced, their common sense and judgment are strengthened.

Unfortunately, a declared goal of our elite technological society is to gain more leisure, not realizing that for most of us this trend is a harsh enemy of creative living. This is one reason Japan now excels us in many respects industrially. We are disposed to kinds of recreation that destroy more than they create. Amusement becomes abusement to our youngsters when it is encouraged in lieu of manual skills, for it generally is indifferent to their most lofty potentials mentally, physically, socially, and spiritually. We have become a spectator society, building cushions on our rears and doldrums in our heads. Except for a curious and creative few who are willing to sacrifice present pleasures for future benefits, television and rivalry sports have largely replaced exploration and experimentation.

Some parents and schools are coming to realize that a head-hand-heart-health balance, so long promoted by 4-H clubs and many schools, produces self-concepts far superior to conventional student activities. And such self-confidence is the key in the lock that opens the door to stable, mature, creative, and productive citizenship. Physicians, lawyers, engineers, teachers, and nurses who have first carefully learned manual trades are better professionals. They understand and respect the nobility of manual labor and that in building self-respect—and therefore mutual respect—the equality of man is clarified.

When we first reported this principle to the 1960 White House Conference on Children and Youth, it appeared too simple and naive for some educators and other leaders to grasp. They seemed unable to grasp a solution that wouldn't everlastingly insist on ever larger budgets and more degrees. It was particularly opposed by some labor leaders. But when they heard that veteran mega-educators like Ralph Tyler backed the idea, a trend toward more practical education began moving with wonderful success in cities like Cleveland and states like California with their garden programs and ROPs.

## The Excitement of Confronting Tradition

Tradition can be a rock-solid base for progress, or it can be a millstone around the necks of families, schools, and society. In twentieth-century American culture, it has become unpopular, even onerous for a child to work. This is one of those senseless, unproductive folkways which, if not curbed, will destroy any society. We don't argue that many children weren't overworked in the old sweatshop days, but those long-ago-outlawed practices should be no excuse today for labor unions and shallow-minded parents to stand in the way of family businesses, school chores, apprenticeships, or manual training programs that build skills.

I was introduced to the harsh and unforgiving bindings of tradition while interim president of a Philippine college. I had been called there from a successful reorganization program in Japan after World War II and was assigned to get the college "into the black and strengthen its accreditation." Yet the horns of tradition poked through our best laid plans one day early in the college year. A powerful member of my board approached me privately in my office. He reminded me first that he headed a large and "successful" church school system and then laid down his opinions of our program with his fist on my desk.

"Do I understand," he asked with obvious hostility, "that your program demands that *every* student [in this college] works every day with his hands?"

"No," I replied, "we make no such demands of any student. The program is entirely elective for fifteen to twenty hours weekly, and we keep tuition at about half that of other colleges and universities. . . . "

"But, but . . ." he started to interrupt me.

"*All* students," I continued, knowing full well what he meant, "*elect* to work when they apply for admission, because *only working students study here.* And *all* teachers agree in writing to work daily with the students and learn to know them outside the classroom. *All* freely agree to 'advance and support' the philosophy, goals, and methods of [this institution] and sign their names, verifying their understanding that their affidavit includes our work-experience program."

"Why on earth do you require that for students who can pay?"

"Please don't forget what I just told you," I responded. "These are neither requirements nor demands, and economics are not our first concern! These students know full well what they are getting into, for we make the reasons crystal clear: First, such a program balances minds and builds character and self-respect, regardless of their socio-economic status; they enjoy a physical and psychological advantage over students who don't have this privilege.

"Second, the students do much better in their studies; they learn to make better use of their time.

"Third, it is proving to be by far the best program in this small college to reduce our debt—as we build services and industries, and that is one of the main reasons I understand I was brought here—to get this college accredited at the master's level and to get it out of debt. I used to be a public school coach and have been one of the most addicted sports fans, but we simply can't afford the elegant sports program some of you have in mind.

"And fourth, balancing study with the work experience helps students understand the equality of man: Whether rich or poor, black or white, large or small, genius or average, male or female, under this plan they better understand each other in a place where such understanding is badly needed—the college."

He was unimpressed at the time; in fact he was fuming. "Well," he retorted, "I'm not going to have my daughters building callouses to satisfy your whims. They're college girls now!"

"I'm sorry," I told him firmly—and gently as possible—"that's policy, and we don't make any exceptions. If we would let one get by, another and then another would quickly make similar demands, and soon the program would break down."

I thought this educator was my friend and would see the plan's logic, particularly as a member of the board which had approved it. But I was wrong. It was all right for other students, but not for his girls.

He kept his word and withdrew his two daughters from our college. But after a few weeks, worried teachers and students reported that he was spending more time on campus that semester than ever; they thought he was looking for trouble. However, our collective puzzlement turned to delight when one day, well ahead of announced registration days, his two daughters appeared at our admissions office to enroll for the next semester. They became some of our best work-study cooperators. All stories don't end so happily, but that was a lesson to me on the sometimes illogical and binding nature of conventional, traditional thinkers. And there is nowhere tradition is more oppressive or can do more damage than in the home and the school.

Nearly every school or school system involved in such programs have faced such opposition. Cleveland's highly successful gardening curriculum failed in part because it was unconventional and dimly viewed by budget makers. Head Start's original and highly-effective Home Start was scuttled because its results ran into the vested interests—and politics—of those who preferred the more showy "store-front" operations. Even California's highly successful ROPs have been repeatedly attacked. And family education plans which involve children in cottage industries for even a half day or so have been viewed with enmity by labor unions who fear their challenge, and also skeptically by neighbors and public and parochial educators as distracting from studies, when in fact they greatly strengthen academic achievement.

Tradition operates in cases such as the town council that refused to install a fence at the top of a cliff, but chose instead to buy a shiny ambulance to pick up the careless citizens who fell over it. Those who make policies are often more willing to put out money to remedy situations which they could have prevented for less money and pain. Manual work is one of the world's most blessed remedies for prejudice, indifference, insecurity, indolence, and delinquency. Rightly approached, it brings love, thoughtfulness, security, diligence, and dependability.

Yet excuses are easy to make, both by parents and schools. This was and is particularly so in Japan where Mark and Athlee Bowman are Evangelical Free Church missionaries. We knew something of the problems they faced, for we had presided over a balanced work-study program in a Japanese college which turned out to be highly successful despite traditions and scholarly prejudices to the contrary, so we encouraged them to quietly ignore convention and give the work experience a try. Athlee summarized their experience in a letter around Christmas time in 1989, a few months after we visited with them in Tokyo:

Talking with you gave us the courage to put into action your educational principles which we knew were true. We've unstructured a lot of the children's educational time. They're learning more by doing and discussing and are becoming more interested in learning. The excess textbooks and worksheets that I knew weren't working, we've dumped.

Also, we stopped giving the children allowances (welfare), and they are earning money by doing the laundry and other extra jobs. At first they were depressed, but the changes that occurred in their personalities were tremendous! They look for work to do, do it well, organize their time, are less bored in their free time and are generally more pleasant to be around. They are earning more money than they got on the allowance system, and they're a great help to me as I go to language school three mornings a week. Overall, I think they feel good about being so competent around the house. I was worried that they would be over-burdened. It didn't happen.

## The Benefit of Inventive Industry

If you are curious about how and why Athlee related "welfare" to "allowances," read on. The human source of this wisdom was a small boy in Kittanning, Pennsylvania. In 1987, necessity being the mother of invention, home industry happened to serve unexpected purposes. Sue Richman was facing problems teaching piano to her nine-year-old Jesse, because Molly, three, was not always willing to play happily nearby, and six-year-old Jacob did not seem to occupy himself productively during those periods. It was sort of a "suspended in waiting-room vagueness," says Sue.

So now she hires Jacob for one dollar a week to baby-sit Molly for the hour she spends practicing with Jesse, provided Molly does not "disturve" (Jacob's word) them, and it seems to have solved Sue's problems. Jacob likes earning money at his job, and Molly seems to feel special and important with her "big" brother's full attention. Both children now look forward to their time together, including Jacob's planning ahead: "Maybe tomorrow," he suggested, for example, "Molly and I could make up a pretend store."

They have built with blocks, dressed up in "outrageous outfits," played pretend games with dolls and stuffed toys, imagined all sorts of dramas, and even baked cookies and muffins all by themselves. Sue says that Jacob is now their creative resident baker, his forte being carob *everything*, with no recipes needed; yet, she adds delightedly, "It is almost always edible." The two little ones laugh and giggle in their new and productive prosperity during this former wasted part of their day.

Jacob has unending creative ideas; he especially enjoys counting and learning about his money and has plans to buy small apple trees for the family's future orchard. He has already purchased a small set of colored pencils for himself. Sue explains that they do not give their boys allowances, yet most routine work around the house is done with reasonable cheerfulness and without pay; but Jacob's job during piano time is extra.

After they recently finished reading a children's book on the history of America's social welfare system in America, nine-year-old Jesse observed that "allowances were sort of like welfare for kids." We think that Larry Burkett, Peter Drucker, and other common sense financial advisors would agree with this wisdom of a child.

# NINE

# THE C-I MAGIC: WHY COTTAGE INDUSTRIES ARE SPECIAL

I t seems that you are in good company if you are interested in starting a cottage industry. Mark Clements Research found that 84 percent of all mothers employed full- or part-time agreed with the statement that, "If I could afford it, I would rather be at home with my children." In 1989, the U.S. Bureau of Labor Statistics estimated that at least 18 million Americans currently perform some income-producing work at home. Nearly two-thirds of these people work exclusively at home, and half of all the home workers work at least eight hours weekly.[1]

Its potential growth is highlighted by economics forecasters who predict that 15 to 20 percent of all the U.S. labor force will be home-based by the early 1990s. Already, since 1980, the number of full-time home businesses have almost doubled and is expected to double again by 1995. A third of all new businesses registered in 1988 operate out of the home.[2] These figures are even more significant when you consider the intensive opposition of labor unions and possibilities of home business failure.

In 1988, L. G. of Tennessee lost her job and was unable to find another which would allow her to be with her children most of the day. Depressed, she was reaching out for almost any comfort or distraction when she turned her radio to Dr. James Dobson and his "Focus on the Family" radio program. A few months later she wrote him this letter:

> Your program a couple of months ago with Dorothy and Raymond Moore has changed my life. . . . I was out of work for six months and couldn't find anything that was suitable for me where I wouldn't be away from my children most of the day. . . . Several months ago, my husband brought home a sour-dough bread recipe and a cup of "starter," and we had been enjoying home-made bread and giving it to friends and relatives, especially during the holidays.
>
> I started going out myself each day with my children and selling it. At that time I was making a batch (three loaves) in the morning and evening (six loaves a day) with absolutely no [capital] investment. I already had my pans and bowls, etc. Then, since I was spending about two hours out at lunch time each day (Monday through Friday), I decided to try another idea I heard the same day on that program—home-made sandwiches. I make egg-salad, tuna-salad, chicken-salad, and ham and cheese. I charge two dollars each. I also had flyers made up, but they weren't necessary because once people saw my fresh, delicious sandwiches and bread, they were sold.
>
> I have quite a repeat business. I average making about ten sandwiches daily and am now making twelve loaves of bread daily. Each day I make about fifty dollars (on Mondays when I have extra bread from making loaves on weekends, I usually have eighty dollars a day). Some days I also make more than ten sandwiches if I feel there's a demand for them. I average making three hundred dollars weekly for about the last month or so. After I consider about forty dollars tithe, then about forty dollars weekly for supplies, that's still quite a profit. . . .

The last time we talked with L. G. she told us that weekly sales were over four hundred dollars. She found an excellent market in selling to real estate agents and brokers, beauticians, and to others who often have to stay at their desks through the noon hour.

She also allowed that she had the typical fears of failure, for she had no previous experience in marketing nor in other business of her own. She had heard our interviews with Dr. Dobson which included a story about single-mother Andrea Geller of Chicago who did well with her early teen daughter, making and marketing sandwiches. Then she, like Andrea, became a classic example of what mothers can do with very little money, but with more than a little determination, imagination, and organization—all three of which we have set out to encourage in this book.

A key reason for including a cottage industry in your children's education is to help them discover the practical need and application of the three R's in everyday living and to provide motivation for learning a bread-and-butter skill or way to earn a living even though they may later acquire another skill or profession. There is no richer way to develop self-worth than in uniting hand with head and heart in building manual skills.

Our emphasis should be less on how to make money than on the relation of work to your children's mental, physical, social, and ethical or spiritual standards. It should make clear that the kind of rivalry that tries to scuttle the competition destroys the golden rule, and that selfless cooperation is as elegant and lofty a goal as selfish rivalry is a lowering path to destruction.

Yet, in at least nine out of ten families, the challenge of home business is more clouded by the possibility of failure than lighted by the excitement of building a profit-making business. These challenges have brought questions to us by the hundreds—in letters, phone calls, seminars, and casual conversations. We will take time here for some of the most often asked and will treat them in more detail as we move on through this book.

## Most Frequently Asked Questions

### What Do You Really Mean by Home Industries?

Reports are flourishing in radio, television, and the press that, with low overhead, home businesses are America's fastest growing work scene, with surprising profits and success. Homes become manu-facturing, sales, and service centers, with profits ranging from a few cents a day selling lemonade to more than twenty thousand dollars annually in Dallas, where the McKim children join their mother in everything from baby-sitting to catering weddings. Oth-ers range from the few dollars a day Rachel Dow, eight, of Roches-ter, New York, makes on her memo calendars, to Andreas Anderson's record fifty dollars an hour when he made computer ROMS in New Orleans. Andreas now, barely of age, runs his own computer business, serving universities and industry.

### What's in Them for Families?

The first answer you may hear is money. But when children are involved in learning how to work, in order to make and manage money, the greatest income may be in character: self-confidence, creativity, frugality, dependability, promptness, and mutual re-spect of a quality seldom seen in families today. They learn man-ual skills, the nobility of work, and how to best use their time. They learn economics and frugality as they apply their math to keeping accounts and write checks for the family utility bills and industry costs.

Almost invariably these students use their time more effectively and make better grades in school. California's Regional Occupa-tional Programs [ROP] report that their high school students who divide their days between work and study average highest in the state in achievement tests. And home-taught children average in the top quarter of the nation. Such manual work has proven by far the most effective antidote for delinquency and drugs. Such work programs out-point conventional "home work" on every score.

### What Can We Make Within Our Financial Ability?

In chapters 12 and 13 you will find a list of over five hundred industries ranging from agriculture and animals to zinnia care and working in zoos. We strongly urge, as Dorothy did to L. G., that you check out your work or service markets, and begin small. It doesn't cost much to make a few cookies or to buy minimal tools to make small wooden toys. Services of all kinds are in astonishing demand. During one visit to Dr. Tim Shepherd and his wife, Virgie, and their family near Dallas, we found two public school teachers with their own children cleaning houses under contract with builders. They found it quite easy, with a system and inexpensive equipment, to make from one hundred to two hundred dollars a day, each.

## But Still I'm Scared. How Do I Begin?

We believe that there are enough stories in this book, with sufficient variety to give you courage, and possibly the most extensive list of home businesses—industries and services—than in any book anywhere. Much depends on you and what you are trying to accomplish. If it is just to keep little youngsters busy, an apple box makes a great lemonade stand in your front yard. If money is your problem and there are many little children and working mothers in your community, child care may provide an excellent source of income. Some women advertise in affluent areas whose families pay more for care and either sit in or have children brought to their own homes.

If you are interested in an industry, check out the needs for the product you have in mind, either local or national. Know your financial limits and stay within your budget. This usually means starting small unless you or your partner, if any, are thoroughly experienced. If you have a partner, make sure your agreement is in writing and complete. Get mature counsel on this. Soon you may have enough volume to purchase your ingredients wholesale. Just don't go so far and fast that you or your children burn out. In one Missouri family, the children, ages six and eight, bake only one day a week. But they can hardly wait for that day!

If you are teaching at home—and all of you are in one way or another if you have children—involve your youngsters at every preparation step. Have them write experienced manufacturers, marketers, business people, families, or others who have been over the road before you. Make sure that they see the obvious rewards ahead—vacations, college, insurance for a driver's license, clothes, spending money, or just food on the table. And as they mature, let them in on your other motives: building character and personality, positive sociability, and worthy citizenship.

## K.I.S.S.

Some think this means "Keep it simple, Stupid." We prefer, "Keep it simple, Sweetheart." But it's easy to be stupid.

First, as best you can, clean up your act: your closets and cupboards, your home (inside and out), your clothes, your car, and your yard. If you have any doubts about your standards, call in a friend or relative who is not afraid to tell you; what seems clean to one person may be unkempt, even filthy, to another. As far as possible, make your home a model in your community. No one in his right mind readily buys from a sloppy source. And if your product is some kind of food and your local health department requires inspection, you will be ready.

Second, become organized, but not over-organized. You need a place for everything and everything in its place. Keep a note pad and use it. Plan your work and work your plan. Set a schedule you can comfortably follow, and learn to put distractions aside. We found our children to be easily distracted; then I realized I was, too. Don't let radio or TV intrude on an accounting job or measuring your important recipe. You can quickly make a costly mistake in putting together a recipe of any kind or cutting a piece of wood too short if your mind wanders for a moment. There is much more on this in chapter 8.

Third, know the rules. One family collected a heavy judgment when their son's hand was crippled for life from a jointer in a high school woodshop. Another received similar sums for loss of a boy's eye from careless school welding practice. If you get into making wooden toys with power tools, be sure you know who is around them. In many states no child under sixteen may be hired for such at-risk jobs. I have known experienced mechanics who lost fingers or limbs by a moment's carelessness. Likewise we mention again the vital importance of cleanliness in food preparation. And be certain your product, whether food or wood, painted or unpainted, is acceptable under local and state statutes. And if your volume is large enough, you may have to charge sales taxes. Don't forget those income taxes, if any.

Fourth, practice common sense. Amazingly few people these days count the cost. Consider those who continue to smoke while friends and relatives all around them are crippled or die from emphysema, lung cancer, or heart disease. Or yet those who eat too much or the wrong things and risk their health, friendships, or marriages by becoming obese. So in business, count your costs! Look ahead and sacrifice present pleasures for future benefits. We operated one business for over twenty years with increasing profitability both in money and influence, yet when another took it over, he shortly had twice as many people doing about the same amount of work and used thousands of dollars for luxuries. The business began losing money and has yet to turn around.

Like Thomas Edison, George Washington Carver, Florence Nightengale, or Paul the Apostle, manual work at home should be less a reason for reluctance than for rejoicing. Abe Lincoln was involved in one business after another and sometimes several at a time, from clearing land and splitting wood to running a grocery and piloting a river boat.

## What Is a Cottage Industry?

It might help to summarize the ideas of this chapter with a quick check list you can use to set up your own industry. Your industry should have these characteristics:

- Something one can do well at home.
- Honorable work, worthy of a good citizen.
- Flexible in hours so as not to interfere with home life.
- Unrestricted by a business hierarchy or labor unions.
- One that provides freedom of choice of work partners.

- Unpressured, enabling you to control your pace.
- Offer as much manual work as possible, including large muscles.
- Simple, yet creative, not requiring expensive equipment.
- Skill-building and challenging, but learned quickly.
- Something, if practicable, that you can pass on to others.
- Something that does not require expensive amounts of space.
- Principled, meeting human needs more than mere wants.
- One that builds integrity, quality, and self-respect.
- One that, if possible, doesn't isolate you from others.
- One that requires minimal initial financial risk.
- Something that tends to restore instead of divide families.
- Something that all of you enjoy.

# TEN

# HOW OTHERS DO IT

A family recently called us, asking for ideas on home industries which would be foolproof—low cost, no failure, no chances of embarrassment, not tiring, but enjoyable and guaranteed to grab their kids' imagination. There are no foolproof industries as long as the human factor is there, and we told them so. Yet we urged them to involve their children in choices of things to do and gave them some ideas. We referred, among other sources, to *Home Style Teaching* where we listed more than two hundred options.[1]

We have learned that when earnest people worry about failure, the best way to allay fears is to share experiences of those who have been over the path before them. We did this in *Home School Burnout,* a book for both homes and schools that shows how many parents and teachers have faced up to rigid conventional education and have relaxed with their children and students to bring out brilliance and powerful characters.[2] We received so many gratitude letters for that approach that we use it again here to reassure you who fear starting an industry. And there are other reasons.

Soon they called again, but this time with quite a different message: "There are so many choices," they laughed. "Now we can't make up our minds." Then they added the real reason for their call. They wanted to know about financial capital, profits, and marketing. But most of all they were curious about people who had successfully carried out certain industries.

So in this chapter we give you sample stories of successful home businesses with comments and helpful details we do not include in our general books. You will share the excitement of many families in their planning, starting, puzzling, enjoying, and otherwise making a business go—and its unifying effect on the family. Our goal is to make you comfortable by knowing how others did it. Notice how on occasion the original industry idea evolved into something different or a variety of industries as parents and children's creativity and common sense were allowed free rein. And in learning any industry or trade, don't hesitate to apprentice yourself or take some lessons from your local high school, adult education class, or other worthy source, as you will notice Jackie Sanders did in making ties. More on apprenticeships in chapter 14.

Here and in chapters 6 and 11, we give you a range of more than five hundred industries and services from which you can make a selection, whether you are rural, urban, rich, poor, young, middle-aged, old, or must reckon with weather extremes and remain indoors for much of the year. When you count these, remember that often a given category such as animal care can include many separate "industries." The total could easily be several times five hundred. But first we give you a story or two of general family involvement.

## Families Can Do It

The Richard and Penny Barker family is into raising goats for milk and raising and training dogs for dogsledding, border collies for working with sheep, raising colored sheep for wool, exotic strains of cattle like Irish dexters, and also not-so-exotic-yet-profitable poultry husbandry. Here are a few short-short stories from animal care to writing, first an omnibus business report from the remarkable Barkers whose basic operation is in Millersburg, Ohio. Penny writes this at our request from their Michigan "cabin":

I can't think of a better place to study the subject [of family industries] than in the Amish communities around this country. In our Ohio Amish community there are *so* many little businesses run right in the home, and the children help more and more as they get older—and of course are around it from birth. There are women who weave rugs, men who repair small engines, entire families that have a tarp shop where they make covers for boats and many other things, greenhouses—many of those, quilting shops, shoe repair shops, harness repair shop; our neighbor makes buggies, and his sons help, and his father had the shop before him. . . .

With my own children there has been Britt [her oldest] selling goat's milk and writing her column for the local paper for five years until now Helen [Hegener] is publishing a series of books by Britt.

Maggie [her second child] began with her colored wool sheep and sold fleeces to people all over, then on to border collies, raising and training them and selling them to people in other states. Now she is into sled dogs, and we have partially paid for our cabin here by inviting others to become paying guests and share in the dogsledding adventure [similar to their Ohio farmsteading program below]. Also Maggie used to card wool for people; she spins her own wool and makes various things from it which have been mainly for our family. She and I also made comforters from wool and sold them at one point.

Dan is in Costa Rica with Britt right now, having earned *all* of the money for both of them from his poultry and from making wooden things on his foot-powered scroll saw. Ben has earned his money mainly through selling Irish Dexter cattle which he raises. All of the children including Jonah do every bit of their share of the work in our farmstead program [taking in children for brief periods to familiarize them with farm life] as well as our dogsledding program. . . .

Maggie, whose creativity Penny lays out so neatly above, is the young woman we describe in our book, *Home School Burnout,* as not learning to read until she was eleven, and within a few months was reading with even better comprehension than her older sister, Britt, who had been reading since she was four. The freedom to create instead of being bound to books or relegated to a special education class through most of those early years is notable here.

In a business which is a kin to the Barkers' farmstead program, Ellen L. of South Carolina offers a hint to those grandmas and grandpas or widows whose children have left home and have left behind empty rooms, which may provide an excellent income. This is particularly true these days, she notes, when some hotels and motels have gone out of the range of some of us common folk. In a recent stay in Williamsburg, Virginia, for a conference, Dorothy and I stayed in a home that was registered with and recommended by the Visitors Bureau. While others in our conference were paying up to one hundred dollars or more nightly, we paid less than twenty-five dollars—to an older couple whose children had homes of their own—for a clean and attractive suite and bath in one of the better areas of town. In Grants Pass, Oregon, we stayed at a most attractive bed and breakfast inn operated by a middle-aged couple at half the cost of local hotels.

Another Millersburg, Ohio, home which offers an outstanding record in both industries and service is Galen and Sadie Miller's and their family of eight. Here, in addition to their report on service experiences in chapter 6, is Sadie's response to our request for an outline of their home industries. Note again the close cooperation of parents and children and the sharing of authority and rewards.

> Our sixteen-year-old daughter is keeping our financial records for the farm and household income and expenses—writing out the checks to pay bills, etc. She's also making baby dresses to sell at a local store on consignment.
>
> Our thirteen-year-old is making a graph record of each of our seventy-some cows to record milk production. She does each lactation with a different color pencil, so we can see at a glance what's happening to their production. Hopefully that will help us cull low producers and problem cows.
>
> For our three oldest, the co-op that sells our milk has a Selective Competitive Quality Program to upgrade the quality of our milk. There is some cost and some extra time involved. But if we can reach their requirements, we can get a premium of

to one dollar per hundred pounds, which we
nay divide if they're willing to do the extra work.
ish Dolls to sell. Our thirteen-year-old wants to
:s for the dolls for a part of the profit. She also
Anging the size of a bandana handkerchief that
Ars at a benefit auction.

-old is learning to crochet. Her goal is to make
an for the Spring Arts Festival that our local
nport group is planning for April or May. She

on to sharing the housework, including the
s, the laundry, baking, cooking, etc. Whoever
iven week to keep the kitchen clean also does

l of America in Davenport, Washington, J. J.
he autumn of 1989. Her report, like those
g and full of ideas and successes that we must
ere. This is not to suggest that every family
activities or businesses; rather it is to verify
ill (motivation), there's a way (method).
children discover this, they love it and are
almost invariably successful. Note the self-sufficiency in these stories and how they consistently distinguish between *wants* and *needs.*
Here is J. J.:

Your latest *Moore Report* just arrived, and the need for input on
home industries/home management caught my eye. I'm hur-
riedly packing to take our eldest to the State Fair. She qualified
to go to state in 4-H Fashion Review by bus, packing our food, as
we are—by the world's standards—poor folks. But I want to stop
before I forget to give you that input. Also briefly to plug the 4-H
program.

I think it is an excellent companion to [our practice of]
home schooling. The materials developed and supplied at low
cost by the local land-grant colleges and designed for teaching
youth in a fun atmosphere are always up to date. We have a
county-wide 4-H club just for home schoolers. . . . It's a great
place for our children to meet and learn to work with other kids
from seven to eighteen.

Older kids are encouraged to take positions of junior or teen leader. We have projects in everything from health and science to animals, plants, and home management. Parents and youth can find out about joining or starting a club or just using the materials, if they are quite remote, by calling their local county [agricultural] extension office. . . .

We live in a remote, rural canyon, beyond the phone and power lines and with a large family and livestock to care for. Here even crafts fairs and other forms of income-producing activity would be difficult. My emphasis then is on home production and self-reliance and developing and fostering attitudes that allow us to live on very limited means. In this regard our isolation helps: We don't have neighborhood kids and TV pitchmen constantly haranguing us and our kids over the latest consumer fad. Our kids grew up with the basic idea that there are no fad or gimmick items, meaning that we don't buy them . . . from Saturday morning TV toys to Mickey Mouse T-shirts to designer jeans. Not that I have anything against Disney or Sesame Street or Gloria Vanderbilt . . . It's just that we drew a line, and there's where it was drawn.

It was an easy one for the kids to see, led to little hassles (everyone knows what gimmick and fad items are . . . whereas if we'd tried to say, for example, Mickey was OK and He-Man not . . . well, you see where that would lead) and has become so ingrained that [the children] automatically follow it. This has enabled us to spend our money on either less expensive alternatives (a six-dollar pair of plain tennies wears just as well as a twenty-six-dollar pair with "Big Bird" on them), or more expensive, well-made classics (like a durable metal trike or huge box of wooden blocks that have lasted through five kids).

We economize on clothing, but we have to manage around severe fiber allergies to synthetics. We sew . . . not necessarily a cheap alternative unless you need 100 percent cotton or wool clothing. That stuff is expensive, but you can find good fabric sales, and we get hand-me-down fabric and clothes from well-to-do friends as well.

To encourage the girls to sew when they reach their teens, we put them on an increased income, but we require them to purchase all their own clothes except for one coat or pair of boots per year; then we offer to subsidize home sewn stuff. You'd be amazed at how well that works—as it has with the State Fair.

We also have a huge garden and grow virtually all our own veggies, storing them in jars and in our immense root cellar. We have no electricity, so we use a rented freezer locker primarily for meat, much of which we grow, also. The kids know if it's June, every meal will contain strawberries; and this time of year the dinner veggie is likely to be corn and tomatoes. . . . Everyone helps plant, tend, and "put by" our food.

Since we live in such a remote location, we have minimal housing costs. Our house payment is 125 dollars a month, plus a few dollars for propane gas for the summer cook stove and winter lights, plus some kerosene and gas for the chainsaw with which we cut our wood for heating, cooking, and water heating in the winter. *We have no electric, water, sewer, or phone bills at all.* What we save by being self-reliant and living in a primitive place—under nine hundred dollars monthly, net—enables us to live as a single-breadwinner family. With Mom at home, the kids are able to participate in a variety of activities that mean transportation to other places like Davenport, our nearest town twelve miles away, or Spokane, forty-five miles for church, 4-H county events, field trips, Mensa youth group activities, and visits with friends.

Not everyone would want to or be able to live as we do, but when faced with the decision about where we wanted to raise our family, we chose the country and were willing to do whatever necessary to reach this goal. We deliberately chose this life as a family, and we are all glad that we did. . . .

Most of these stories have been told by parents, so before we go on to our short-short descriptions of successful home businesses, we think you would be interested in a report from a current teenager. When asked to speak to Seattle's home school graduating class of 1988 at Pacific Lutheran University, I found myself facing thirty students with unusually high scholarship for high school students, based on standardized tests; but even more remarkable were their work experiences, including management and/or sub-management of chain eateries like McDonald's and Fish 'n Chips, and a number who ran their own industries. One of these was Dawn Cunningham, then fourteen, who consented to put her story in writing now a year and a half later. Here is part of her story:

> At about the age of seven, I started designing and making hair ribbons for infants through adults. Later I started making corsages. I would go door-to-door (with an adult) selling the ones I had previously made and would also take orders for those who wanted them custom made. My parents don't believe in allowances, so I did this for extra spending money. One particular day I . . . made twenty-two dollars and fifty cents in thirty minutes.
>
> When I was eleven, . . . I started taking classes on First-Aid, First Aid for Infants, etc. These classes helped me to get private baby-sitting jobs and my first job in a daycare. I worked one day a week for ½ day, for three years in that job. At the same time [I was] doing weekly daycare for local churches during their Bible studies and most recently with my thirteen-and-a-half-year-old brother, and did daycare for Crisis Pregnancy Center on a regular basis.
>
> At age fourteen I began doing some bookkeeping and on-the-job work for Thorsett Landscaping. I do everything from office work to taking inventory to weeding and digging.
>
> At age fifteen [after graduating from high school] I also started teaching piano, and now at age fifteen-and-a-half I also work for Eastside Escrow, doing filing, answering phones, and a lot of other paper work. So in essence I have three part-time jobs . . . but try to work only between fifteen to twenty hours per week, because I am going to GRCC (Green River Community College) full-time, in fact finishing my first year this quarter [February 1990].
>
> In case you're interested, I'll tell you a little about some of the things my four brothers are into. We buy huge bags of popped popcorn [available at many discount houses], and my four- and nine-year-old brothers bag it into brown paper bags and put all the bags in their wagon and pull the wagon around the block, selling the bags for twenty-five cents. They always sell out!
>
> If they sell half of the large bags, it not only pays for the entire bag (our family eats the other half), but gives them spending money, too.
>
> My thirteen-and-a-half and nine-year-old brothers are becoming quite talented at working with wood. For about a year now they have been building picnic tables (children's size) with at-

tached benches, also planter box wells. They sell those items at twice what it costs to build them. The planter box wells sell for fifteen dollars each; the picnic tables range from twenty-five to forty dollars. They sold well in the summer and, surprisingly enough, people even stopped by to buy them for Christmas presents.

I have used earning money as a learning tool in home schooling, also. One of the requirements was that I keep a ledger, figuring out the percent of profit on different projects, then dividing my money into different categories. I've always had to put 50 percent in savings, the other 50 percent was divided amongst tithes, gifts, clothes, horse, and activities.

I'm certainly glad I put that 50 percent in savings, because so far I've paid for all my own college tuition and books. Someday I'd like a car and insurance so I can help my parents with all the driving they have to do—driving me to and from college—and all five of us to music, etc.

## So Many Kinds

Including unpaid services of chapter 6 and the long list of successful home businesses in chapter 11, we take you rapidly here through nearly forty short stories of successful cottage industries, for we have found that this is the single best way to allay your fears and make you comfortable in starting a new business, whether industry or service.

## Aquariums, Birds, Reptiles, and Things

Madelyn Camp reports that her family has for the past several years bred and raised zebra finches, guinea pigs, rabbits, cockatiels, hermit crabs, hamsters, turtles, kittens, dogs (Labrador Retriever), a boa constrictor, and tadpoles (raised into frogs) "literally leaping out of the aquarium in the living room!" She describes fourteen-year-old Amanda's cottage "industry" as combining scholarship with teaching. Amanda actually offers both industry and service.

Spending her own money, she has been using microscopes, ordering sheep's brains, hearts, and eyeballs and sharks from a biological supply house to study and dissect. She studies and teaches art and science, charging three dollars per lesson for art and four dollars for science for a total of about one hundred and fifty dollars monthly in addition to two hundred dollars over a two- to three-month period for art work and shows.

## Animal Care and the Super Scoopers

After buying an eighty-acre farm, the Ron Bradshaw family of the British Columbia, Canada's beautiful Okanagan Valley, decided to introduce their children to animal care.[3] They chose first to build a flock of sheep and raise horses and ponies, along with raising hay and grain to feed them. When Jenny was twelve, she bought three sheep with her savings and cared for them entirely herself, although she shared her fun with Nicky, ten, and Thomas, three. Jenny learned about delivering lambs on cold spring mornings, and after her "midwifery" duties, learned the "pediatric" care of newborns and ewes, and has become Nicky's mentor and example.

They train horses and ponies for other families as well as their own. Their earnings pay for their horses, and with the training they carefully give, they are able to obtain top prices for their animals. This has led to Jenny's and Nicky's participation in fairs, horse trials, and shows. Jenny was even asked to be a groom for the British Columbia Teams at the National Horse Trials.

## Raising Colts with Love

The following letter illustrates yet another example of one family's unique approach to raising horses.

> We felt quite a tug on our heartstrings as they loaded our two new purchased colts in the horse trailer. The colts were only five months old, and they had to coax the mothers in the trailer in order for the colts to follow. After the colts were safely loaded, they shuffled the mothers quickly out of the trailer and slammed the doors tightly shut before the colts could dash back to their mothers' sides. The conversation between the colts and their mothers' as the truck slowly faded into the distance towards our

home was enough to bring tears to the eyes of the most hard-hearted individual.

We were somewhat inexperienced with raising horses, yet we decided we were going to love these precious animals just like the household pets of cat and dogs we had adopted in years past. At first they appeared quite cautious and even nervous around us, but they quickly developed a kinship with our children, Alyssa, age ten, and Nathan, age nine, who were very devoted in their time and attention to each of them. We discovered each colt responded very much to our affection and definitely had their own individual personalities and identities. *Goldie,* our palomino mare, loved to eat, was very responsive to cooing and cuddling, and was a little bit lazy. We were surprised to discover that, when talking to her and brushing her, she often started to sway and plop to the ground with very heavy eyes. Alyssa and Nathan would plop down with her while continuing to coo and brush her until she was asleep. They would lay with her and against her while we would snap pictures of them. *Skippy,* our sorrel stallion, was a different story. The neighbors often commented that he would surely make a race horse as he loved to run and run *fast!* He was and continues to be quite playful—loving to tug on Goldie's tail and mane and mine, I might add. Yet in the evening when all the running and playing was completed, he had lots of love to share. Skippy liked to put his nose close to ours and breath deeply and then lay his head on our shoulders as if to say, "Boy, I needed my hug today."

We've had our colts only five months now, and Alyssa and Nathan can ride them bare back in the field, and the colts are quite comfortable to have a saddle placed on their backs. Recently, Benny McClerron, the man from whom we purchased the colts, came to visit and was shocked to say the least when he saw Alyssa and Nathan crawl up on their colts. He said, "I have never seen colts act so tame in all of my years of dealing with horses." We recently became acquainted with Kenneth Jackson who has been raising horses for about thirty-five years, having a farm of over one hundred and fifty horses, and who also travels most weekends to judge horse competitions. He came to visit one day and expressed his shock also as he said, "I guess I won't have to worry about your kids around these colts anymore. I have never seen anything like this, and I will have to bring my movie camera over to get this on tape so my colleagues will believe it!"

In talking to many experienced "horse people" and in doing a little research on the subject, we have discovered that the standard philosophy in raising horses is to basically leave them alone until they are two years of age or older and then "break" them into obedience. If you have ever witnessed a horse being broken, I'm sure you will agree this is very difficult for man and animal. We have found that most of God's principles addressing the treatment of our fellow man apply to the treatment of animals also. Just as God's love for us is the most active power in changing our carnal nature into the divine, so is love the most active power in molding sweet and responsive dispositions in animals.

Animal care of many kinds—both small and large animals—is a common home business, including animal sitting during client's vacations, grooming, feeding, and cleaning. Many earn by cleaning stables, but the young boys in one enterprising Minnesota family have organized the Super-Scoopers who at a good rate of pay accomodate city dog owners by cleaning dog droppings from their back yards.

## Auto Body . . . and Other Industries

When Dave Whitaker was twelve, he apprenticed in Iowa in a trade which is now his family industry, and is apprenticing his son Joel, fourteen, and three of his young friends in his own Kirkland, Washington, auto body business. For years his daughter Janet, now eighteen, handled the office, including reception, telephone, and cleaning. It prepared her for an employment agency job in Redmond.

> Janet and Joel's mother, Suzanne, is proud: [The boys] begin by cleaning, washing cars, and removing masking tape and paper from painted cars. Then they learn to do the masking and start buffing cars and taking out some of the simpler dents. It takes about four years to learn the trade well. Two of the boys plan to go to college next year. Whether or not they end up doing body work for a living, this is a skill they can fall back on if needed.
>
> The boys see . . . men working in harmony and overcoming difficulties in a way that shows respect . . . for one another. They

learn to value diligence, responsibility, and honesty. If a customer is dissatisfied, they learn integrity by seeing that the customer is satisfied or his money is refunded. Once when one was dissatisfied with a nine-hundred-dollar job, Dave refunded him one thousand dollars! One time a man left a five-dollar bill in the car to test their honesty; the boys added another five dollars to test his!

Suzanne also reports that Joel helped her sew little dolls a few years ago when he was ten. He made one dollar on a four dollar doll. Now, from that introduction to sewing and his involvement in car repair, he is considering becoming an upholsterer. And her daughter, Bonnie, nine, learned dependability last year by raising and selling tomato seedlings. She had to plan ahead and miss some events because she had to care for the plants every day. (We add here that one kindergarten class in Western Springs, Illinois, made about three hundred dollars yearly by planting tomato and flower seeds in cookie tins, caring for them every day, including weekends, and when they were ready, transferring them to half pint milk cartons, in which they eventually sold them.)

## Baking Bread

Literally thousands of families make others happy by delivering a best seller—homemade bread. We are connoisseurs of homemade bread, and some of the best in the world has been placed before us, baked by children as young as six and eight years old. Our dearest bread bakers are our grandchildren, Bryon, ten, and Brent, seven, in Virginia, and nine-year-old Jessica Reinmiller of Portland, Oregon, and her oldest brother, Jeremiah, age eleven, although even little three-year-old Daniel gets in on the action. Their bread is as professional and delicious as any that Grandma ever made!

Located in between are Laura Freire and her family who make a genuine business of bread baking in Tennessee. She writes:

My children and I have opened a bread baking business—thus far two afternoons a week, but with a plan to expand to three days. If anyone tells you it is impossible to knead twenty loaves of bread at a time by hand, don't believe it, for it is done in this home. We are keeping our eyes open for a good used twenty-five lb. mixer, but until then, by hand it has to be. We have a pizza-type oven that handles twenty loaves at a time. To put less than that takes on a loss.

I am doing as you recommended by incorporating the children into different facets of the business. Indeed I almost gave up the venture until I did [take your advice], for the load was too great. Now the boys take turns baby-sitting, and when they're not watching the baby, they are oiling pans, sweeping, bagging, etc.

I am starting to make rolls now and am teaching them to form them. I must not leave out Elizabeth. She helps with most things, too. Eventually I want to start teaching them the bookkeeping end of it. Of course they receive a salary—a quarter a load, which right now comes to a dollar a week—big time to them.

Laura is fortunate to have a commercial oven; most families who bake bread use their own kitchen stove. A mixer is a handy device, a work saver that assures consistent kneading.

Arlene Cook's three children, then twelve, ten, and eight, made bread and rolls, selling them first to relatives. The children decided what they wanted to bake and sell and learned markets in the process. Their father helped them figure how much it would cost to make each item and establish the mark-up for profit. They then designed their flier, which involved writing and drawing, and ran them off on their father's copy machine. The children handle all the sales transactions.

## Catalog Store

In Pennsylvania, Mary Trembles and her family operate a Sears Catalog Store near their home. Their pre-teen children have learned to run the cash register, including complex adjustments, taking orders, filing them, putting away shipments, checking on freight deliveries, and writing up merchandise returns. They are delighted with the many learning experiences for the children in this small business.

## Peanut Butter

The Barker children in Texas are getting business experience by purchasing peanuts from their natural foods co-op and selling peanut butter which they make with their Champion juicer.

## Raising Pet Rabbits

In Illinois the Lesly Parkers decided on a pet rabbit business for their children ages eight, five, and three because it is easy, quickly developed, and provides a lot of hands-on experience. They first went to local fairs, talked with breeders, whom they found to be friendly and ready to share expertise while looking over their stock. They obtained pamphlets and books from their County Extension Office and library and started with mini-lops. They build hutches of wood and mesh wire and enjoy the cooperation of feed stores and nearby breeders. They discovered the value of registering their animals with the American Rabbit Breeders Association.[4] And they studied rabbit reproduction (thirty-two days), pricing, and many other unique things about these furry little creatures.

## Paper Routes and the Brandt Industries

Craig and Carol Brandt's four children all have paper routes. The older three are up at 5:15 A.M. daily, and the five-year-old has a weekly shopper route she runs with Carol's help. Their earnings take care of their extra needs—clothes, spending money—among other things. Their older daughter won two trips through coloring contests and recently received two hundred and fifty Disney video cassettes which she is using to open her own video rental business. Last year their son Trevor raised fourteen hundred dollars for the Multiple Sclerosis Read-a-thon with one hundred and twenty sponsors. For two years the Brandt family also ran a stationery business. And these hard workers excel in achievement tests.

## Greenhouse

Teenager Mitchell Ross became interested in carnivorous plants. Then from one of our articles, he says he got an idea for a greenhouse. Now he has a full-blown business he calls Mitchell's Greenhouse and sells seedlings, bedding plants, and hanging baskets. His profits are already ranging from twenty-five hundred to thirty-five hundred dollars yearly which he plans to use for college.

## Muffins

Joel and Daniel Varnods, eight and seven, are excited about their new Hungry Bear Good Food Company. They make four dozen bran muffins at a time which fellow employees at their dad's office claim priority purchase. Their next project with their father is making birdhouses.

## Pet Store

The Hansen family of Augerties, New York, have opened a pet store in an old train station across from their home. Their thirteen-year-old daughter can run the store by herself when necessary. She and her seven-year-old brother feed, clean, and care for all pets, including varieties of reptiles, mammals, and birds, and price and handle stock. The three-year-old boy keeps the kittens and ferrets happy; both boys carry bags for customers. They like the idea of chores, income, and fun all in one.

## Recycling

Kristy Carey, seven, has run a recycling business for three years. This includes newspapers, glass, cardboard, aluminum, and plastic bottles and jugs. She's learning math, money management, and common sense along with ecological priniciples of energy and waste. (For details on recycling, see chapter 5.)

## Drive-In Restaurant

Walt and Jolene Catlett find their daughters Cara and Jana, thirteen and twelve, excellent helpers in their Nebraska drive-in eatery. Even eight-year-old Joshua and six-year-old Joel do well servicing the parking lot and caring for other chores. "Since we started helping," Cara says, "we all understand Daddy's job better. We got upset when he didn't come home on time, but now we know that he can't always leave at a set time." Jolene observes that the children not only enjoy handling money responsibly—and learning a lot of math in the process—but are discovering the importance of respect for older folks. Walt sees a trade as a great challenge, trading Jolene's services in the restaurant for the children's help, so that Jolene can spend more of her time mothering.

## Easel and Chalk Board Manufacturing

For several years, Carla Banks and her Iowa family have done well financially, building chalk boards, marker boards, cork boards, and easels. When their largest distributer, a Colorado Springs catalog house, called recently with another order, the proprieter was moaning that he was a month or more behind in shipping orders. Carla and her children saw in this an opportunity for "doing things for others" which balances the materialism of industry, so she offered to bypass shipping charges, bring the things he had ordered, and "all five of us, ages thirteen and up" spend a week helping him get caught up. The man was delighted. For a week, two of her home-taught kids worked in retail, quickly learning what was in stock, and what was not, running the computer accounting system, adding up bills, figuring percentages on discounts, counting money, running the laminating machine, and learning customer relations in general. She adds:

> The rest of us filled our one week's "apprenticeship" restocking shelves, filling orders, and doing secretarial services. The owner was grateful and astonished at our "efficiency." We went home happy and educated, not expecting a dime for the experience, but a week later there arrived in the mail a letter of very high

commendation and sizeable checks for each of us. Don't over-look apprenticeship programs as part of your training!

## Energy Store

In New York, Ed and Karen Schadel join their children in operat-ing a wood stove and fireplace parts store where they specialize in energy economy. First, twelve-year-old Joshua read the instruction manual of the new cash register and practiced its functions which he then taught his parents. The children do everything from wash-ing windows, cleaning, pricing, and shelving merchandise, assem-bling accessories as needed, answering (and screening) phone calls, relaying information, and answering customer questions. Even Caleb, two, began sorting change into the proper compart-ments at the end of the day, and learning that the "total" button was the one to push to end a sale.

## Sitting Services

For about ten years, the Sullivan Sisters Sitting Service has been serving the Orlando, Florida, area. They are neither ordinary baby-sitters nor do they limit their home industry to sitting. They, like many, have diversified into a variety of services and industries. But the point we want to make here is their system and standards. They started out with a neat pink calling card with a little stork on it. They have their own phone call pads for messages to their cli-ents when they return home. They realize that a lot of sitting is sloppy, TV-oriented, and basically irresponsible. They set a better example.

## Pumpkin Patch and Squash Field

John and Julie Wasser have three children: Tait, sixteen; Carrie, twelve; and Zach, nine. Minnesota's *Stillwater Gazette* became in-trigued with Zach recently when he came in to place an ad. Zach is involved in a variety of industries with his Northwest Airlines pilot father. But this time he wanted to sell pumpkins and offer his services as a sort of caterer, taking decorative corn stalks and pumpkins to local businesses to spruce up their places for Thanksgiving. Zach specifically asked his mother to home school him so that he could be a businessman. Sometimes he makes sales; other times he barters, as when he traded a bundle of stalks for a cinammon roll, lemon bar, and a scone. That day he split with his dad—who also drives the pickup truck filled with Zach-grown pumpkins down to the corner where Zach takes in up to twenty-three dollars from pumpkins in an afternoon. Such reaping follows a lot of weeding, an hour or so of planting (five seeds to a mound) on Zach's half acre of soil just south of the chicken coop.

Villa Lenz reports that her family first went to local fruit and vegetable stands to establish their market for a squash-growing project, although as they became known, they later also sold to private buyers. This is a lesson for all garden projects lest you make the mistake of one boy and rent an acre for growing carrots and then find that you can't sell them. The Lenz's made it a family project to study how best to work the soil, fertilize, plant, and water. It was great fun to watch the plants sprout, grow, bloom, and bear squash. They raised about three thousand pounds of ten kinds of squash of which 1,750 pounds went to the vegetable stand at ten cents a pound, and five hundred pounds to private buyers at the time of their report.

## Furniture Making

Paul, eleven; Tim, ten; and Joel Alme, eight, are involved in a variety of projects, ranging from expanding their basement to installing an intercom system and building their own seven-drawer, solid oak executive desks. They saw desks like those they made advertised on special for 399 dollars. Their cost per desk was eighty-five dollars. As Joel speaks for these brothers (including Shane, fifteen, whose apprenticeship we describe in chapter 16), note not only the manual skills learned, but also the character lessons and the worthwhile involvement of a highly skilled retiree, age eighty, whom the boys met through his second vocation—haircutting:

We were involved in a woodworking class this year. Our teacher was our barber, and he has a shop in his basement. He is retired now, and he used to teach woodworking at Verona High School. He made my mom take the class, too. We like woodworking, and we like Mr. Johnson! He is very kind to teach us.

We learned to identify wood types, and [we] used oak, walnut, cherry, birch, ash, and mahogany. We learned how to sand and use different stains and sealers. We used many hand tools, including a center-finding rule and clamps of many sizes.

We learned safety as we worked with the machines. We used the band saw, radial saw, bench saw, jig saw, router, drill press, planer, bench sander, and electric drill and screwdriver.

We also learned to take care of things right away and how to clean up the shop. We made napkin holders, knife racks, step stools, cutting boards, plaques, [a] mirror, and trivets.

We are very thankful for Mr. Johnson and proud of what he has taught us!

## Breakfast Food

Seven-year-old Jacob Cusack of Ada, Michigan, searched with his mother for the right business "for at least a year" and came up with the idea of making a breakfast food much like the famed Swiss Mueslix. Jacob sent us a generous sample—his common marketing practice—with this flier that covers just about all questions except calories:

Hi!

This is a free sample to introduce you to a cereal I am selling. It is very good for you as you can see from the list of ingredients (listed by order of amount):

Whole wheat flakes, rolled oats, oat bran, raisins, walnuts, wheat germ, brown sugar.

Just pour some milk over top for a tasty breakfast cereal. It is similar to the Swiss Familia cereal that sells in the grocery for three dollars per twelve ounces. I am selling twenty-one ounce bags for three dollars. Does that seem high? Let me compare a few prices for you.

- Cheerios 20 oz./$3.00
- Honeycomb 10 oz./$2.25 (or 20 oz. for $5.00)

- Five-grain Mueslix 14.1 oz./$3.35 (or 20 oz. for $4.75)
- Swiss Familia 12 oz./$3.00 (or 20 oz. for $5.00)
- JACOB'S FAMILY 21 oz./$3.00 (or 20 oz. for $2.86)

I hope you enjoy my cereal. If you'd like to order some, just give me a call or stop by and I'll make sure you get it!

JACOB CUSACK

P.S. If you like hot cereal, mix ½ cup of my cereal with ¾ cup of water and cook for two minutes and twenty seconds on high in your microwave.

## Haircutting

This may not be an appropriate trade as a regular business, for it is carefully controlled by health authorities. Check your local and state statutes on this. But in the Moore family, Dorothy has been our barber for many years, with cash savings running into the thousands of dollars, from a capital investment of a few dollars for a good pair of barber shears and comb. She seldom uses our electric clippers any more. When we started, I had my doubts, and still realize that not all parents can do this, but it is a skill that most can develop, and stands you in particular stead when you live far out in the country or have a restricted budget.

## Label Collecting

Many kinds of collecting are available as home industries. In the case of service-oriented Holly Driscoll, eight, of Washburn, Wisconsin, it is Campbell Soup Company which offers a variety of rewards for labels. Her very large goal for a little girl is to earn a Dodge Maxi-Wagon for her school. She has enlisted help from a wide variety of sources, including the press. The September 5, 1989, *Family Circle* reported that she had already collected 60,000 of her 975,000 goal.

## Wood Toys

Jim Lamieux of Graham, Washington, tells us that he services over a hundred arts and crafts fairs in Washington State alone, selling wooden toys. He told us of a listing of such fairs in his state by *The Bunnie's Guide for Artisans and Crafts.* And of course there are the telephone yellow pages. He agrees with us that wooden toy making offers very good profits, particularly if the toys are creative and simply made. He is a woodwork teacher and shares our conviction that with very little skill most people can do it.

## Computer Software

Matthew Wright, age nine, with his father Randy, are owners of Matthew's Mississippi Micro. They sell public domain and shareware computer programs of which few laymen are aware, yet they can save the computer buff a lot of money. Their capital investment has totalled one hundred dollars plus Randy's computer.

## Seasonal Industries

Melody Hylander's Hylander Industries in Jackson, Mississippi, bakes and sells sourdough bread at Christmas time. In springtime, handcrafts take over—ladies' scarves and collars, girls' hairbows, and Victorian fans. And year round, Melody sells Discovery Toys. (For some years Ruth Canon of Dallas has operated a similar industry.)

## Custom Dog Food

The Charles Loorman family of Reno, Nevada, makes custom dog foods in cooperation with the veterinarians in their area. They follow vitamin, mineral, and other prescriptions, and specialize in making nutritious, customized hard-baked dog bones. They say anyone can do it. See also chapter 15 on this industry as a solution for learning disabled children.

## Shopping Service

In classifieds around Palm Springs, California, you may run across one of Mari Palmer's ads. One that we saw runs like this: "ARE YOU TOO BUSY TO CHRISTMAS SHOP??? Tired of fighting traffic!!! Let us do it for you!!! Mari's Shopping Service." Mari charges fifteen dollars for a grocery trip; ten dollars for a Christmas or other present, and five dollars for each extra up to three, two dollars and fifty cents each, over three; and provides receipts for all purchases. This may sound prodigal to some, but by the time average shoppers drive their cars for such errands and place any value on their time, it makes sense for many. Mari says that many clients use her services for holidays, and most are "ordinary people" who are too tired at the end of a long day to go shopping. "What makes this great for me," Mari tells us, "is that I just love to go shopping!" That might give you a clue if it's for you.

## Beekeeping and Other Things

When he was thirteen, Norman Cary discovered two beehive swarms hanging from an abandoned semi-truck bed near his home. Cautiously, he put them into boxes and brought them home. Six years later he was in the industry full-time, using the bee business to put him through college.

Today at thirty-three, Norm is one of the larger apiary operators in the nation, with more than forty-one hundred bee colonies spread over ten California counties, from the central California city of Modesto, in the San Joaquin Valley in the north, to Redlands, located in San Bernardino County in the southeast which he operates with large trucks. He centers his Cary Honey Farms operations at his Lindsay, California, farm.

Bertha Goettemoeller of Brashear, Missouri, also promotes beekeeping as "a profitable industry" for homes, but on a much smaller basis than Norm Cary's. In *Families for Home Education* she advises you to get in touch with your local state university extension office as a first step.[5] "Then check books and farming magazines at libraries [or find] a neighboring apiarist (beekeeper)" who will "certainly know the scene." Many home educators are full time beekeepers. Bertha counsels to remember cleanliness in gathering and storing honey, and suggests co-ops and grocery stores as markets. She also notes that "properly-packaged honey stores indefinitely, and producers selling from their homes soon have repeat customers."

## Quilting

Mrs. Goettemoeller also recommends quilting. Apprentice yourself to an expert or take a class or read a book. There are many markets, including shops, galleries, and interior decorators. We add that a certain amount of creativity is helpful here, and, well done, this industry is for the patient worker. It has also been a boon to many shut-ins. But be careful about pushing it too soon and too much with small children—under age twelve—whose eyes are yet immature and who, like even older children, need large muscle activity much more than the fine muscle movements of sewing. We don't say "None at all," but think first of children's needs.[6]

## Garage Sales

Laurie Langdon reminds us in *The Bulletin*, which Meg Gallina publishes for home educators of Treasure Valley, Idaho, that conducting garage sales is an excellent industry. Our friend, Marceil Moore, did this for us when we left Michigan, and it was successful, a real service, and a great relief to us. You must usually be in a position to help provide sound pricing and be dependable and reasonably well organized. You may contract to handle a given garage sale on a commission or other basis; you may be selling for one family or a group. But if you handle it well, you can build a reputation quickly and keep busy. It is an excellent way to build up capital in a business, for it requires little or no capital itself.

## Desktop Publishing

In the first issue of the *Home Business Advisor*, July 1987, Jane Williams and others headlined desktop publishing, noting that it can "mean everything from a profitable business . . . to a money-making sideline, to a way to generate your own brochures, forms, newsletter, letterhead, and even catalogs."[7] In short, it might provide an excellent service to other home industries. Using the proper equipment—computer, laser printer, etc.—you can design almost anything in print. If you develop skill (and we reemphasize the proper equipment), you can serve business and industry in your area with an excellent profit. Take care to approach several computer organizations, so that your work is not straitjacketed by a single viewpoint. IBM, COMPAQ, Apple/MacIntosh, and others will likely serve you well.

## Sign Business

Steve and Marilyn Hodgin of Mize, Mississippi, share a sign business with their sons. The boys prepare boards, stack silk-screened signs, and use their sign computer (see Desktop above) to cut out letters for jobs. The day Marilyn wrote us, the boys were finishing a four-hundred-dollar job with the computer. Their older son enters the words to be cut, and the younger one "weeds" out the background.

## House Numbers

Some dear Texas friends of ours who don't want to be identified first gave us the idea of painting house numbers on curbs. Many have used this device for excellent profits. Usually they make up a little bracket which they can place against a *clean* place on a curb (which is neither wet nor very cold) and insert the correct numbers into the bracket and spray with a can of appropriate spray paint. Some have used a letter punch and separately punched out each house number, but that is more costly. We suggest that you check with your paint store for the most durable paint to spray on concrete. And depending on your price—five, ten, or fifteen dollars—you may first spray an oblong area in a background color, and use a contrasting color for the numbers. Most often black and white are used. You may also want to specialize in custom designed house numbers—on boards, metal plaques, or figures—and charge appropriately. Some towns may require you to check first with them.

## Picnic Tables

This harrowing genesis of a home industry with its descriptions of pitfalls and near-failures is too good to adapt or paraphrase, so we tell it in the words of its author, Ron Duncan, quoting from the *Home School Journal* [8]:

> Our family tried for two years to find our very own cottage indus-
> try. We tried raising chickens to sell to stores; but most grocery
> stores want U.S.D.A.-certified chickens. So we bought another
> flock of chickens. This time they were layers. We later discovered
> that the eggs needed to be inspected and certified for sales to
> supermarkets.
>
> We then decided to buy some goats and sell the goat milk,
> and that was more disastrous than the chicken industry. The
> goats had to be state certified and the milk tested, and the "ole"
> goat barn [had to be] cleaner than the Mayo Clinic . . . [except
> that] we weren't required to wear masks or rubber gloves when
> the boys and I milked! We thought since our home school is not
> certified by the state, why should our goats and chickens be? . . .
>
> While working in Omaha, Nebraska, as a semi driver, I've
> been able to meet a lot of people in different businesses. One
> man I know is manager of a large refrigeration service for [re-
> frigerated trailers]. He asked me if I wanted or could use some
> wooden crates or pallets. They were made of 2x4 and 2x6 boards
> seven feet long. I told him yes. Why, I'll never know. Each day on
> the way home from work, I would stop and pick up a load of
> pallets until we had stacks and piles of pallets in our yard. . . .
>
> We really didn't know what to do with them until my wife
> Connie said, "I wish you and the boys would buy me a nice pic-
> nic table before summer."
>
> We looked at those wooden pallets with a new idea, with a
> new vision, and started building picnic tables. My wife can now
> go out in our yard and pick almost any tree to sit under and
> there she'll find a picnic table.
>
> We have since sold picnic tables to a large lumber company
> in Omaha and have become their supplier for picnic tables. We
> have built over a dozen tables in our one-month-old cottage in-
> dustry. . . .

## Chalk Business

Wendy Priesnitz reports from Canada about a Colorado family
whose only product is sidewalk chalk.[9] It is run by Suzanne and
Ross Greiner, eleven and eight. The two wanted to earn money to

go to Disney World, and they asked to start a home industry like their mother was running. Now they market the chalk through manufacturers' reps, fundraisers, and direct mail order, and are investing for their college educations. Their mother says:

> They have gathered a wealth of knowledge running their own business; everything from what we do when someone doesn't show up to work on time, to being computer literate to process their orders, to learning how to ship international orders, and most importantly, how to keep going when you would rather do something else. They now have employees to help them. . . .

## Rubber Stamps

Ginger Mackie tells us that her daughter, Laura, then seven, discovered rubber stamps and brightly colored ink pads. Because of her interest, the Mackies bought her some. With some ideas from her father, she started making bookmarks, gift enclosure cards, and postcards to market in their local rural area. The shop owner suggested the possibility of finding remnants of card stock cheaply at a local print shop. So now Laura does quite a professional job on quality materials. She deals with local business people, provides receipts, and is learning the responsibility of keeping shops supplied with her cards and bookmarks. And it's been great for the family!

## Deli

Kristi Jacobsen, now fifteen, has become a key operator in a successful Barrington, Illinois, delicatessen which was started by her aunt and her mother. The cooks say, "Kristi is our best worker!" And customers wonder how she can laugh and sing when it's her turn to wash the big pots and pans. One asked, "What did you do to make her love to work?" Her mother, Noreen, reports that family industry and giving authority equal to her ability to accept responsibility is the key. Kristi has already won a number of prizes for her cake decorating—an asset in businesses that often cater weddings and parties.

## Economist-Conservationist

Eric Kebker, age nine, has a daily job walking a neighbor's dog for five dollars a week and manages his own money. When he saw a Genoa, Ohio, billboard ad about Christmas Club savings, he headed straight for the bank and opened an account on his own. Now responsibility is catching on with his six-year-old sister, Melissa, who solicits neighbors for their cans. Melissa provides them with containers, collects them when filled, cleans, and crushes them—returning "nice, clean" containers to her customers. With her last recycling paycheck, after tithes, she bought an outfit for her gymnastics lessons.

## Tie Making, Scarves, Table Cloths, Lingerie, and Similar Things

Some of the most swank and best tying ties I have were made—or remade—by Jackie Sanders, who, with her husband Paul, lives just south of Yosemite National Park, California, and usually winters near Palm Springs. Such an industry offers a perpetual market and excellent profits year around if you are an excellent seamstress or tailor and have a sixth sense for patterns that sell. We have had enough requests for her recipe that we are giving it—and some other valuable ideas—to you here in Jackie's words:

> Several years ago in a yardage store in Fresno, California, I found necktie material at four dollars per yard. After thinking about it for several days I went back to buy some of it and found it marked down to one dollar a yard. So I purchased two yards, and my husband liked both pieces. A week or so later at another yardage store operated by the same company, I found more— and a larger variety—of the material on sale for sixty-nine cents a yard. The material was forty-two inches wide and when cut on the bias, there is enough in one yard to make three ties. So first, select your material carefully, and be careful how you buy.
>
> Next, I bought a good tie pattern, the lining or "tie shape," and I started making neckties. The main principle is to be absolutely sure the ties are cut on the true bias, otherwise they will not hang or tie right. The lining or tie shape (also cut on the

bias) is important as the tie will not hold its shape, and it will wrinkle.

A necktie should never be pressed completely flat, but should have a slightly rounded edge. If pressing should be necessary, a piece of ⅛ inch plywood, cut in the shape of a necktie and covered with cloth, can be inserted in the wide end of the tie and carefully pressed (If plywood is not available, a piece of firm, thick cardboard may be used). Thus you don't run the risk of pressing the edges flat, or having the seam on the back of the tie show through on the front.

Rules for tie making:

1. Proper necktie material.
2. Material cut on a true bias.
3. Tie shape for lining, also cut on true bias.
4. A good pattern. If it is made of tissue paper, transfer it to heavier paper.
5. A good-sized table on which to cut material.

If there is difficulty in finding a pattern, an old tie of proper length and width can be dismantled and used for a pattern. I found Simplicity #8785 for long ties [once called "four-in-hand" ties] and bow ties. Another may be Vogue #2826. Currently the costs will probably range from four to six dollars. And don't forget to find a good quality of lining material!

Recently I have been remodeling ties that are too wide, to a narrower width, and it has worked very well. A lot of nice ties were given to me. I laundered them, remade them, and they all turned out very well.

My grandmother taught me that "a woman who sews, her fingers are gold." I make all my own lingerie, robes, etc., as well as ties. By careful shopping I have found lovely lace at five cents a yard and nylon tricot 108 inches wide for one dollar a yard. I bought enough to last for a long time because the price might not be the same tomorrow, especially the way prices go on a woman's slip these days. And how about the market for nighties, scarves, and table cloths? Generally, none of these are too complex for you to make.

Most of us don't wear hats very much any more, but there may be a market here, too. Years ago I went to a millinery class where I copied a forty-five-dollar hat for five dollars, including the velvet.

And children's clothes can be very expensive, yet they don't take much material and are quite easy to make. Choose simple patterns at first, if you are a beginner. I learned to smock dresses and to sew lace on the edge of a collar to eliminate the need for double thickness and to improve its looks.

I have found that home-made clothes usually wear better and longer because they are made better, and that happens when there is pride in accomplishment. You may make a lot of mistakes if you are a beginner, but don't we all? Just learn from them. With a good sewing machine—not necessarily a fancy one—and a good pattern and materials, you can accomplish a lot.

## Free-Lance Writing

We have found enormous talent among parents and children who are writing for everything from *Family Circle* to *Guideposts* and *Reader's Digest* and a variety of newspapers. They range from such imaginative and skillful writers as Linda Dobson in New York and Mary Pride in Missouri to Kathleen Creech and Nancey Pearcey in Washington. And they are not limited to America. From Australia, Suzie Hammond tells how she got started:

> I decided, after a fortuitous accident with a bookcase in the library, to do some free-lance writing (The aforementioned bookcase dumped two very interesting American books into my lap on the subject of making money by writing for free-lance markets). . . . I have taken their advice and so far have sold one story to the largest newspaper in Australia, *The Sidney Morning Herald*!! My first brainstorm was an article titled "What you and your kids can do about the Educ Depts new cutbacks"—the minister is firing teachers, putting more kids in each class and then repairing falling down school buildings with the dollars he saves. This has some parents really upset.
>
> Over here the Journalists Union . . . suggests a pay of $358.20 per thousand words. Not bad pay, but it's not steady unless you have reams of ideas going out to various periodicals all the time. I thought that since I don't want to get a 'real' job, do want to keep home schooling and need to be able to make dol-

lars in odd hours when I am not flat out with the rest of life, free-lance writing should be perfect. I have several ideas out to other magazines and one go ahead for an article in home schooling. It's wonderful to get paid for something I really enjoy.

Mark and Laurie Sleeper not long ago sent us a complimentary copy of their new journal *Home Sweet Home* which featured writing and contained many key pointers for the beginning author.[10]

We might add as authors or contributors to more than sixty books and several times that many articles, ranging from scholarly journals to *Reader's Digest*: Write like you talk. Then write, write, write! Ask for criticism. Expect it. When it is given, use it! Remember that even the best of authors usually have an ample collection of rejection slips. Remember also that it is oftentimes more difficult to make truth attractive than it is fiction. Even though much modern editorial policy is slanted or expedient, *whenever you depart from strict integrity in writing or in editing, or fail to thoroughly research the recommendations you make in your books or articles, you are in essence dishonest and risk hurting your reader.*

## Significant Communal Efforts

Other than the Amish, one of the most exciting groups of families involved in cottage industries sponsors a series of communities under the auspices of the Truth Forum. They operate under the general guidance of Blair Adams, Joel Stein, Howard Wheeler, and other highly-principled men and women in Colorado, Texas, and other states. I visited their Koinonia Children's Craft Fair Exposition at their Rehoboth Ranch near Crawford, Colorado, at the same time as Texas attorney Curtis Brown and his wife were there. It was not hard to see that these people were not wild-eyed adventurers. Many, perhaps most, of them are business and professional people who have tired of city life in such places as Boston, Chicago, and New York, and are seeking a peaceful place to rear their families. We agreed that their crafts, ranging from wool carding to blacksmithing and from lace making and landscape painting to food preserving, were some of the momentous educational demonstrations of our lives.

The sheer unconventionality of such programs as the Barkers and the Truth Forum sometimes makes them the object of conjecture or the butt of ridicule. I was called to witness when one of their families was hauled into a Delta, Colorado, court because of their "strange" operations. Yet I was unable to find a single neighbor around Rehoboth Ranch who did not have a good word for their orderly and productive operation. One of these days when the rest of us are enjoying our modern "luxuries" and we suddenly find ourselves without water, electricity, and gasoline, the idea of having one's own garden and even plowing with giant horses as they do at Rehoboth, will begin to make a lot of sense.

With ecologists warning that disaster is ahead if we don't come to our senses and be a little more practical, we might well see the writing on the wall. One of those writers is Alvin Toffler who predicts in his book *The Third Wave* that decentralization of the workplace is the next adventure of Western culture. Educated estimates hold that, barring heavy political pressures by powerful labor unions, more than five million familie are now involved in family industries or will be within the next five years. That should be welcome—and challenging—news to you and me!

# ELEVEN

# A FEW HOME BUSINESSES

Since 1947, we have been involved in home or school industries of one kind or another and have for most of those years been publishing lists of businesses we knew were successful in homes and schools. No two families, however, have precisely the same problems. Some are rich, others poor; some are city folks, others suburban; and still others rural. In most cases, though, exciting home industries have brought together parents and children as few other activities can, proving that families who work together stay together.

You can find lists of industries in many books. Those we list in the following pages have enjoyed success in recent years with families of our acquaintance, operating out of their homes. Although it is the longest such list we have seen, it is far from comprehensive, for no all-inclusive list exists. There is no end to possibilities for cottage industries as long as humans have imaginations, wants, and needs. Each item listed below has been a separate industry in one family or more, although, as with animal care, one family may carry on a number of these "businesses." Some categories are so closely related as to force us to be arbitrary. For example, classify-

*185*

ing holsters, billfolds, and belts either as crafts or manufacturing, or tying quilts as "crafts" or "sewing."

And one additional caution: Occasionally sources, such as we sometimes provide below, go out of print or out of business. We have no way of being certain that you can find them, but we suggest that if you can't find them in your own bookstore, you check with your public or university library. You quickly see how many different jobs or industries can develop when you look under "animals, birds, fish" and realize that just boarding animals may be a business in itself, not to mention caring for birds or fish as separate jobs. As you go through this list, don't decide on the first industry or service that catches your fancy, but go through the entire list, then decide on the one which makes you most comfortable and seems most likely to promise success. You can always add others later, as most successful home industrialists do.

## Agriculture

One of your best low-cost sources for information in these areas is your county agricultural agent, who also has state and federal resources at hand. Then you have the state and U.S. forestry authorities, not to mention pet stores and others who are in these businesses and are delighted to share their wisdom and experience. As we suggested before, go to your local bookstore and to your nearest librarian.

- Animals, birds, fish
  - Board
  - Breed
  - Buy/sell
  - Chickens
  - Eggs, friers, etc.
  - Clean stables, aquaria, cages, etc.
  - Clean back yards
  - Exotic animals, raising and selling
  - Irish Dexter cattle
  - Llamas

- Food
- Beef, veal, etc.
- Groom (see also "Services," later in this chapter)
- Train (see also "Services," later in this chapter)
- Vacation and other care
- Walk or other daily care

- Bees
  - Honey packaging/sales
  - Pollination contracts
  - Shipping

- Christmas trees
  - Raising in garden or farm
  - Wholesaling
  - Retailing

- Dairies
  - Cows
  - Goats

- Gardening
  - Bedding plants
  - Fruit (melons, berries)
  - Herbs, mushrooms, domestic
  - Herbs, wild
  - House plants
  - Gathering natural special purpose plants
  - Long rice
  - Mistletoe for Christmas
  - Moss for florists
  - Pumpkin patch
  - Seedlings (flowers/vegetables growth and sales)
  - Vegetable growing and sales

- Greenhouse
  - Growth of tender plants requiring protection from elements
  - Production gardening of exotic or out-of-season vegetables

- Irrigation systems

- Landscaping

- Lawn and garden care

- Nursery stock
  - Reforestation (tree planting)
  - Shrubs (sub-contract growing)
- Sod farm (lawn grass)

## Construction

Here again, go to your local county agent, librarian, and those experienced in these areas. But we especially suggest that you get in touch with your community colleges or state universities whose architectural, engineering, or vocational specialists are usually interested in helping sincere seekers. If you are doing any local building, it is wise to contact your local or county building authorities in the event it may be necessary to obtain building permits and building inspection. Your librarian will guide you in obtaining excellent current magazine and book information.

Especially if you are interested in buying and fixing up houses, it may save you a lot of time and money in the long run if you watch similar jobs closely or offer your services as an apprentice or volunteer. Building techniques have changed astonishingly over the last twenty to fifty years, yet there are engineering and aesthetic principles that never grow old. Don't ignore such magazines as *Popular Mechanics, Popular Science, Mechanics Illustrated,* and any number of helpful how-to-do-it house and furniture journals.

- Cattle guards and chutes
- Feeders (animals or birds)
- Fences
- Houses
  - Building
  - Buying and fixing up
- Mobile home renewal/repair
- Storage houses

## Crafts

There seems to be an endless flow of books and magazines on crafts, ranging from Mary Mulari's *Designer Sweatshirts: How to Trim and Alter Sweatshirts* to Edith Flowers Kilgo's *Money in the Cookie Jar.* Here again, go to your librarian and to home economists at your county, community college, or other college or university. Don't overlook the many crafts people and stores already in the business.

- Badges, identification cards
- Basket making
- Cards
  - Birthday
  - Christmas
  - Valentine
  - Verses
  - Other
- Ceramics
  - Customized
- Glass blowing
- Glass specialties
  - Painting
  - Stained glass windows/pieces
- Illustrating
  - Greeting cards
  - Magazines
  - Books, etc.
- Knitting
  - Sweaters, stoles
  - Hats
  - Baby clothes, booties
- Leather articles (see also "Manufacturing and Repair")
  - Billfolds
  - Belts
  - Purses
- Lamp making

- Macrame and wall hangings

- Mobiles, for babies' beds, etc.

- Nature craft, shadow boxes, etc.

- Paintings
  - Ceramics
  - Silks, etc.

- Pillows, customized

- Pottery

- Puppet making

- Rag rug braiding

- Sewing (see also "Quilts")
  - Alterations
  - Draperies
  - Dressmaking
  - Ties, scarves
  - Slip covers
  - Shell craft

- Silk screen painting

- Woven wall hangings

## Foods

You can hardly find a popular home magazine or woman's journal these days that doesn't feature recipes. But watch out, for some of them that tout low calories are not nutritionally sound and appeal more to fancied tastes and appearances than to your health. If you want truly reliable recipe books which lead to good health, consider the Weimar Institute's *Recipes from the Weimar Kitchen,* Muriel Beltz's *Cooking with Natural Foods,* and Lucy Fuller's *Whole Foods for Whole People.* If you can't find them in your local book store, send a self-addressed, stamped envelope (SASE) to the Moore Foundation, Box 1, Camas, WA 98607.

If you get into baking or making cakes, candies, cookies, jams, jellies, pastries, and pies, you can distinguish yourself and build a unique market if you try to make your products healthful. Some entrepreneurs do this by using fruit juices as sweeteners and more dried fruits and nuts in their contents. Many mothers feel safer with this type of sweet for their children. Let health be your goal in preparation of all foods, and you and all concerned will be blessed.

- Baking
  - Bread
  - Cakes
  - Cookies
  - Fruit cakes
  - Muffin specialties

- Candy making and sales

- Catering

- Dog food/biscuits

- Drive-in or homestyle restaurant

- Family cooking to go out
  - Complete meals
  - Desserts
  - Main dishes
  - Salads

- Frozen foods

- Grains (rare varieties)

- Health foods
  - Dried fruits
  - Manufacture (sprouts, analogs, etc.)
  - Restaurant
  - Store/deli

- Jellies/jams

- Lemonade, etc. (roadside or park)

- Peanut butter

- Pickle making

- Pizza

- Popcorn/confections

- Recipe testing

- Sandwich making
  - School lunches
  - Businesses

- Soups

## Health and Individual Care

We caution you to study health areas carefully before you become deeply involved. They involve the welfare of human beings and are closely watched by local, state, and federal authorities. If you have any questions, check with your local or county health department or with experienced entrepreneurs. Convalescent care, nursing homes and hospices, for example, are overbuilt in some areas, and many are poorly run. Find those which *are* exemplary and study them carefully.

There is a plethora of holistic programs, weight reduction systems, and nutritional advice. We urge you to check out anything you do here against the most proven of medical authorities. This is not necessarily your local physician, as good as he may be, for many physicians are not as familiar with all programs.

- Care, personal/institutional
  - Retirement
  - Convalescent
  - Hospice
  - Nursing
  - Retarded
  - Handicapped

- Foster home

- Health conditioning
  - Arthritis

- Atherosclerosis
- Diabetes
- Heart
- Massage
- Weight

- Addiction
  - Alcohol
  - Drugs
  - Smoking

## Manufacturing and Repair

Some of these programs, like making wooden toys or yo-yo's (at the end of this list), require very little capital, while others, like auto body repair (near the head of this list), require years of experience and should not be entered by any but experts who have very high standards. Yet there are even facets of this trade where beginners can help, as you read in chapter 12.

But it would be wise to study carefully for greatest efficiency. If you are patient and look around or follow the ads, you do not necessarily need to buy new equipment to start an industry. Oftentimes retiring carpenters or other craftsmen or cabinet shops or even estate sales list quality, low-cost used equipment. The principles of skill, creativity, efficiency, frugality, and safety apply to all successful manufacturing.

- Aprons
  - Household
  - Industrial

- Auto body repair/painting

- Bee shipping containers ·

- Birdhouses

- Bookbinding

- Braided items
  - Bull ropes

– Dog collars and harnesses
– Lassos and whips
– Mohair and nylon reins
– Ski ropes

- Broom and brush making

- Camper seats

- Caning (chairs, etc.)

- Canvas products

- Card holders

- Chalk boards/easels

- Clothing and shirts (specialized)

- Computers
  – Making ROM's, etc.
  – Repairs

- Door mats

- Dolls
  – Manufacture
  – Dresses
  – Collecting
  – Repair

- Embroidery/silk screening
  – Blouses
  – Shirts
  – Sweat shirts
  – T-shirts

- Fire wood
  – Cutting and splitting
  – Selling
  – Delivering

- Fishing flies

- Garden carts

- Gates (and gateposts)
  – Electric

- Metal
- Wood

● Hat making

● Hay aprons

● Horse equipment (see also "Leather")
  - Covers
  - King blankets
  - Trailer mats

● Kids' stools

● Leather items
  - Collars of all kinds
  - Cinch covers and chafes
  - Gloves
  - Harnesses of all kinds
  - Holsters
  - Rifle slings
  - Straps, halters
  - Vests
  - Whips

● Massage tables

● Miniatures (room furniture, etc.)

● Mittens (and cloth gloves)

● Motors, electric, etc.

● Neckties and scarves

● Picnic tables

● Picture frames and glazing

● Plaques (metal, plastic, wood)

● Quilts (commercial production)

● Rings and buckles (trophy, etc.)

● Ropes
  - Leashes
  - Ski ropes
  - Tow ropes

- Rubber stamps

- Rugs
  - Hand weaved
  - Loomed
  - Rag

- Sandals

- Scratch pads

- Spinning
  - Mohair
  - Exotic wools, etc.

- Split shakes and shingles

- Tops, spinning

- Window boxes and grow boxes

- Window screens

- Wooden toys

- Yo-yo's


## Merchandising

Merchandising, and specifically marketing, belongs to nearly all items in all sections of this chapter. We caution against plunging into some attractive industry without careful thought to your markets and advertising—whether you will sell door to door, through friends, via church or other bulletin boards, newspaper, radio, and TV. Most successful home industries cater more to needs and wants of their communities than to their own personal enjoyment. And we remind you of what my father always told me: If you put out the finest quality, you need worry far less about advertising. We don't say that the world will flock to your door, but you will have a better chance that they will come to you before they'll buy something shabby.

- Books and educational games

- Chalk sales (varieties)

- Computers and software

- Cooperatives

- Educational tools and toys

- Energy store (fireplace equip., etc.)

- Firewood business

- Food and garden sales

- Flea markets

## Services, Paid

Here again common sense principles apply. The person who is thoughtful, orderly, clear in planning and working his plan and skillful in carrying it out, has a running start over the one who is thoughtless, careless, inaccurate, or unskilled. This applies from accounting to yard services, but let's take answering services as an example, for just yesterday, as we write this, we had five experiences.

We were doing business with highly-reputable offices, but the first three left us wondering what kind of manners govern. We were kept unnecessarily long or forgotten on the phone (particularly disconcerting when we are paying long distance charges), or a second person came on the phone to help us who knew nothing of our call, and we had to repeat the whole message, or the receptionist or answerer simply didn't know anything about the business she was in. These experiences motivated me to make a fourth call—to our own office—to thank our ladies for their ever courteous and informed answers. They may make a mistake, but not often. And Dorothy and I are grateful. After that I had occasion to call the publisher of this book. The response was quick, friendly, businesslike, accurate, and organized to the last jot and tittle. What fun to do business with them! When they promise to call back, they do. When they say they will send something, they will. And without delay. Thoughtfulness is the key—of every detail. No wonder they are so successful at marketing.

- Accounting
- Animal grooming and training, including seeing-eye dogs and other service animals (see chapter 13)
- Art appraisal and consulting
- Beauty shop
- Bed and Breakfast (Inns)
- Bookkeeping
- Brake drum turning
- Child care
  - Family day care
  - Play group
- Cleaning
  - Annual cleanups
  - Automobile washing/detailing
  - Box cars
  - Carpets
  - House or apartment
  - Houses under construction
  - Office
- Chores at school
- Clothing
  - Alteration
  - Reknitting
  - Repair
- Computers and word processors
  - Desk top publishing
  - Programming
  - Service/repair/sales
  - Telecommuting
  - Word processing
- Cooking classes

- Counseling
  - Educational
  - Financial, income taxes, etc.
  - Marriage
  - Psychological

- Designing
  - Dresses
  - Houses
  - Interiors

- Errand running

- Furniture moving

- Games for parties

- Garden
  - Maintenance
  - Planning and guidance

- Garage sales

- Gifts
  - Wrapping
  - Gift baskets

- Guest room rental

- Hair cutting

- Holiday servicing
  - Greetings (mail and other)
  - Parties, etc.

- Hospitality services

- House sitting

- Interior design

- Janitor services

- Lessons/tutoring
  - Art
  - General (see "Tutoring")
  - Languages
  - Music

- – Sewing, etc.
- – Swimming

- Mailing services

- Manicuring

- Music
  - – Accompanist
  - – Dinner music
  - – Soloist
  - – Vocal ensembles (chorus, quartet, trio, etc.)

- Newspaper clipping

- Organizing ("clutter control")
  - – Closets
  - – Cupboards
  - – Homes
  - – Offices

- Painting
  - – Furniture
  - – Interiors
  - – Exteriors

- Paper routes

- Relocation counseling

- Rototilling

- Secretarial (see also typing, etc.)
  - – Personal correspondence
  - – Business correspondence (see "Telecommuting")

- Shoe polishing (drop-off or pick-up and delivery)

- Shopping services

- Sitting
  - – Baby
  - – Handicapped
  - – House
  - – Pet

- Snow shoveling

- Stuffing envelopes
- Telephone
  - Answering services
  - Wake-up services
- Tractor work
- Travel agency/services
  - Tour organizing
  - Travel management
- Tutoring (see "Lessons")
- Typing
- Wardrobe management
  - For adults
  - For children
- Yard Work

## Miscellaneous

The same comments apply here as in merchandising and services. Some of the miscellaneous categories are hardly distinguishable from services. Most are in fact sales or services. Please forgive us if our arbitrary classifications do not mesh with your perceptions. These are the ways they looked to us.

- Antiques
  - Procure and sale
  - Repair and refinish
- Architectural assistance
  - Doll houses
  - Homes
- Coupon and label retrieval
- Copying tape recordings, etc.
- Dry cleaning and/or laundry
- Employment agency

- Exercise classes
- Fashions
  - Boutique
  - Shows
  - Counsel
- Fire fly retrieval and sales
- Flower arranging
  - Fresh
  - Dry
- Framing pictures and mirrors
- Garage sales
- Gift, yarn, or fabric shop
- Golf ball retrieval and sales
- Interviewing
- Kitchen planning
- Magazine subscriptions
- Mail order selling, catalog shop
- Multi-level sales rep
- Nurse registry
- Packaging
- Paint mixing
- Painting restoration
- Party favors and decorations
- Party menus
- Pattern maker and tester
- Photography
- Public relations
- Public speaking
- Recycling of all kinds (see chapter 5)

- Rocks and minerals
  - Decorative
  - Exterior walks, walls
  - Installation
  - Retrieval
  - Supply

- Rubber fencing (from tires)

- Sanding furniture

- Stencil making

- Taxidermy

- Translating

- Upholstering

- Wigs
  - Dressing
  - Making
  - Selling

- Window shades

- Writing/editing/marketing
  - Advertisements
  - Free-lance
  - News
  - Publicity
  - Speeches

We repeat: This list is not exhaustive, nor is the list of free services in chapter 6; rather they are for your information and to challenge your imagination. The possibilities in cottage industries in the next ten to twenty years is almost endless. Some home businesses have even done their own LBO's (leveraged buyouts) by obtaining financing for small commercial organizations which they could operate at home, or the remainder of a home business which they started in partnership. There is something for almost everybody.

# TWELVE

---

# FINDING MONEY FOR YOUR INDUSTRY

I n the Moore household, we have nearly always started with what we had, with an exception, perhaps, in buying our first house or first new car. But let's take a garden project as an example. Sometimes it was a dollar or two for garden seeds or a few cents for telephone calls or postage stamps to obtain advice. We sometimes grew our own tomato or flower seedlings instead of buying three tomato plants for a dollar.

There are few experiences in the world more exciting for a child than planting and waiting and watching for the seeds to sprout and the plants to grow. Yet if you are a beginning "green thumb," you may find buying plants better simply because you are more certain of the results. This is so with almost any project which requires money.

## Credit

There was a time in our lives when Dorothy and I rightly thought it necessary to borrow. That is the only way most of us must go these days to get a start. By far most of the big money is made—

205

and often lost—that way, and that is the basis for a considerable part of our economy. But most of us are either not inclined or not in a position to take such risks.

The chances are that unless you are going into a large business or have been successful enough to justify taking out a loan, you will feel less pressure if you possibly can pay cash and avoid debt. If your children, for example, want to go into car washing as a home industry, as many do these days, they need not buy expensive power equipment, at least at first. Simply dig up enough money to buy a high quality chamois and some strong brushes, then use the family bucket, rags, hot water, and detergent for washing, and a garden hose (preferably with a quick-control nozzle for their convenience).

Once again we say K.I.S.S.—keep it simple, sweethearts (women or men)—when setting out on an industrial program. If you don't believe this, read in the papers about all the men, young and old, whose businesses have failed or who have been arrested for evading taxes or other fraud. In nearly every case we have noticed extravagant living, spending, and other ego-expanding activity. If you are going to be successful and want to avoid debt, you must be prepared to sacrifice something!

If, as is generally the case, you only need a little money to start, and you simply don't have what it takes, you might try a close friend or relative. Otherwise go down to the bank for two things. Money is second, not first. The first is advice. We know of a number of children—as well as adults—who have done this with considerable success. Some of these young bankers are highlighted elsewhere in this book. A child's credit will, of course, usually depend upon his parents' credit. Yet some bankers have more faith in some children than in some adults.

You may, with sound experience behind you or excellent counsel at your side, wish to embark on a substantial home industry, one which has the possibilities of reaching far beyond your home. One of our friends in Iowa, a regional sales manager for batteries, decided that he wanted to be closer to his family, so he decided to go into lawnmower and tractor sales and service. Another young man, a door-to-door book salesman, also found his work taking too much of his time away from his young family and began a whole-sale book distribution business. Still two other thoroughly-experi-enced young publishing executives decided to step out on their own. Such ventures are not only meat for banks, but also Uncle Sam's Small Business Administration (SBA).

We do not suggest troubling the SBA for underwriting a tiny loan. It isn't worth either yours or their time. Although we have never gone this route, we would be remiss in omitting ways to fi-nance a small business or service organization if you are qualified and have no other means of getting started. But whether or not you ask their cooperation on a business loan, they are an excellent source of counsel which can cost you heavily if you go to fee-charg-ing professional consultants.

Notice, when we refer to the SBA, we use the words "under-writing" and "cooperation." This agency does not hand out money, but advises and, if it sees merit in your proposal, guarantees up to 90 percent of your loan. Its limits for any one new business is 750,000 dollars, and its average loan amounts to about 175,000 dollars. The first thing SBA officials will ask you to do, if you haven't already done it, is to go to the banker of your choice for advice, mentioning that you are, or will be, in touch with the SBA.

If you think this will be a typical federal transaction with hun-dreds of pages of documents as I had to process as a federal edu-cation officer, forget it. The SBA—and the banks—want a short, simple statement of such facts as your purpose; market potentials, documented if possible; operational methods; payback plan; your business qualifications, if any; and collateral (or security) to sup-port your loan.

It's unnecessary to go further into SBA operations here, for they will supply you thorough information with little or no cost. Among the attractive ways they are ready to help you are the following:

- A toll free line for all states except Alaska and Hawaii: 800/368–5855. If you are in the Washington, D.C., area, call 202/653–7561. For Alaska, Hawaii, and territories, you may call 202/653–7561 or write The Small Business Administration,

1441 L Street, NW, Room 100, Washington, D.C., 20416. Plan to be patient if you choose to call, for the lines are often busy. But be persistent.

- Catalog No. 115 of publications from the above address.

- Seminars across America, without cost to you. Your local SBA office can keep you posted on dates.

- SCORE. This is a Service Corps of Retired Executives who have rallied to help beginning entrepreneurs and who form a volunteer staff in all kinds of businesses.

- OWBO. This Office of Women's Business Ownership works through local schools and community colleges to offer courses relating to small businesses. They also will be found in each local and regional SBA office.

## Investments

We decided to leave this near the end, yet it is by no means least in importance. We will only lay down several crucial guidelines here. You will soon see why. The investment business is for experts, not for novices. We have seen many lose their shirts overnight, and we made mistakes in our early experience that could have been avoided if we had taken wiser counsel.

First, take a careful inventory of all your assets, in cash, in personal and real property, and any other possessions which should be added into your total net worth. Notice we said "net"—the amount you are worth after all debts have been subtracted or paid. Be honest with yourself and your advisors; don't exaggerate.

Second, decide on your financial objectives on the basis of where you are now, and where you want to be a year from now, and twenty and forty years from now.

Third, select one or more successful business people who have a solid record in a variety of investments, such as real estate, stocks, bonds, money-market certificates, Treasury bills, and listen carefully. Whether you deal with a banker or a broker or other investment type, check out your advisors credentials thoroughly, and be wary of the high-pressure types.

Fourth, keep your eyes open and your ear to the ground for investment prospects which you can try against your advisors. That might sound like a difficult posture, but it may bring you the best returns in the long run. Don't wait for their initiative in all your financial outreaches.

Fifth, the words may be old-fashioned and appallingly trite, yet you can do no better than to plan your work and work your plan. If it looks as if you may be stretching yourself, and you are inexperienced in private business, pull back before you start. Take only as big a bite as you can chew thoroughly, and then take time to masticate. A meal well digested is best for your health. A business approached wisely and with goals of highest quality is your best guarantee of success, and of the faith of others in your operation—parents, relatives, banks, brokers, and possibly the SBA.

## Investing for Long-Range Security

We don't propose an in-depth course in investments, but we offer a few experienced cautions which, although they may not make you rich quickly, will at least help you avoid the pain of financial disaster.

First, don't invest at the cost of your family's health, that is, to drop that monthly savings check do or die. Yet careful planning does mean a certain discipline and family self-control. How to make money and help you on these deposits is laid down in chapters 10 and 11. But remember that your physical and mental health are essentials for prosperity.

Second, have a clear financial philosophy. As a Christian, for example, you may tithe, a Biblical practice important to stewardship.

Third, establish both general and explicit goals based on your philosophy. You may be one who places present comforts first, or you may prefer a sacrificial posture in the interests of future security and retirement or a home if you are now renting. You may consider children's college education more important than buying a home or suffering with an old car a little longer in order to build up your savings.

Fourth, whatever your investment plan, don't put it off! Begin saving early, obtaining the best interest rates and other advantages possible, without unreasonable risk.

Fifth, decide how much risk you are willing to take, given your family's security as the bottom line. Don't believe all those get-rich-quick stories; if it sounds too good to be true, it probably is. Recently Dorothy and I were invited by apparently reliable people to invest for an annual return of around 40 to 50 percent instead of the 8 or 9 percent we were receiving on some certificates of deposit. Something told us to go slow; and we are glad that we did, for the basic investment was shortly found not only to be unsound, but its operators were indicted criminally. Take careful counsel; know which investments are secure, and how their record stands. Generally the low risk investment will also bring the least returns.

Sixth, be willing to diversify. Don't put all your financial eggs in one basket. This rule is followed by nearly all successful investment counselors.

Seventh, don't expect big results overnight. Some counselors suggest dollar-cost averaging over the long term and investing a certain amount regularly. Seek counsel on this. Shop around for advice and settle on a counselor whom you sense is honest and has your welfare in mind.

Eighth, and last, be honest in all your transactions and check out your investments to be sure that they are not run by con-artists. Pay a just tax and do it on time. This doesn't mean that you shouldn't save every legitimate tax dollar you can. Study the tax laws; seek professional help if necessary. Just remember that you have obligations to both God and country.

# THIRTEEN

# WHEN THE HANDICAPPED BECOME ASSETS

I n August of 1989, we met with a dedicated group of home educators in Hilo, Hawaii. They were a practical lot, doing all kinds of things to make ends meet; and they apparently were fairly successful, judging from their optimistic behavior. But no individual or family could match the enthusiasm of Larry and Olga Krejci, a blind couple who live with their six—soon to be seven—children in Puna of the Hawaiian Beaches area of the big island of Hawaii. There they have their home, gardens, and a shop where Larry does arc welding, furniture making, and carries on an active ham radio program.

## Physically Handicapped?

Larry operates power saws and other machinery regularly, yet still has all of his fingers on both hands. When I expressed surprise, even astonishment, he laughed at my naivete. He has trained seeing-eye dogs and does some obedience training, house wiring, and minor plumbing such as hot water heater installation, toilet replacement, and sewer line cleaning. He is teaching his sons—Sean, thirteen; Isaac, eleven; and Abraham, ten—electronics and plumbing and has them working on their ham licenses.

He and Olga proudly report that they teach their children at home, and the three boys all test out several grades above their norms. Sean has a paper route in addition to his other activities and is considered mature enough that next year he will receive a driver's license—a privilege the State of Hawaii occasionally grants to children of handicapped parents.

Larry has made a fine bed and cedar chest for Olga and has welded together his own antennae and tower for his ham radio. All of which gave me some new insights on who is handicapped and who isn't. I have since philosophized that he who is handicapped in spirit is more to be pitied than he who is troubled in body.

## Learning Handicapped?

Jeanette Axelrod was handicapped in neither body or spirit, but she did have two somewhat limited sons. When she sought to enroll the third of her eight children in school, the principal cautioned her: "If you put your son in the public school system, you will have to do battle for him. And it will never let up."

Kenny Axelrod was handsome and healthy. At three, he could ride a two-wheeler, but he had not developed language skills. At five, he was diagnosed as irreversibly learning disabled. "We'd been told the limits to his educational potential, and after an awful period of what I'd describe as mourning, we accepted that," Jeanette says. "But I could *not* accept the limits of the education available for such children."

Just as Kenny settled into his first school year, Jeanette gave birth to another son, Howard, who had similar, though milder, disabilities. "I knew I'd have to fight twice as hard," she says. Her first battle was to get a physical education program for Kenny and the thirty-one other special education students in the district.

At home and at school, Kenny's physical exuberance was a force to be reckoned with. One of the few times Jeanette let her determination dissolve into tears was the night she found her baby grand piano in the center of the living room.

"Kenny had moved it there," she says. "He was only ten, but he was five feet tall and weighed a hundred pounds."

Besides his physical strength, Kenny's hyperkineticism, expressed in constant, random motion, was exhausting for the rest of the family. "While other mothers were prying their kids away from TV, I prayed for the day he'd have the concentration to watch just one show.

"After the piano incident, we decided to get him a set of blocks. Cinder blocks. We bundled him up and sent him outside and said, 'Build a firehouse, build a parking garage.' He loved it—he was out there all winter."

By spring, the cinder blocks were worn down to sand, and Kenny was calm enough to watch TV.

"That was a turning point. I'd gotten over the depression, the frustration," Jeanette remembers. "But it was anger—outrage—that kept me active in Kenny's and Howard's schools."

At the outset of their fifteen years in the Lower Merion, Pennsylvania, school system, the then-superintendent told Jeanette that not much was done for special education students, since "they" simply drop out eventually. "They" were afforded no art, no music, no vocational training, no interaction with other students—"they" were even forced to take meals separately.

"Lepers were never more isolated," Jeanette says. School administrators came to dread her visits, but in the end, "they" got a physical education program, a high school program, a vocational director, and, after Jeanette's final battle, the special education students graduated in caps and gowns—with diplomas.

As Kenny graduated and Howard prepared to enter high school, Jeanette realized that her sons' higher education—including economic independence, self-respect and self-reliance—was a curriculum she and her husband, Budd, a family physician, would have to invent.

She asked Budd if she might take the money they would have spent on the boys' college education and start a business they could be involved in. "It had to be something the boys and I enjoyed," she says. "We're animal lovers—always had dogs, cats, Easter chicks that actually lived."

After research, a short apprenticeship with another manufacturer, and consultations with veterinarians and nutritionists, Jeanette was ready to launch Mother's two pet food stores in suburban Philadelphia. A balanced mix of beef and chicken organ meats, cheese, corn, wheat, brewers' yeast, garlic, buttermilk, and wheat germ oil, the canned and kibble forms are now selling in Mother's stores and in supermarkets, kennels, veterinary clinics, and pet stores. Kenny and Howard, now twenty-seven and twenty-two, mix, cook, and package the food. A third son, Danny, thirty-one, takes care of the business end.

When they started the company in 1976, Jeanette bought a six thousand and five hundred dollar piece of food processing machinery for one hundred and twenty dollars at an auction. In order to help them pass their drivers' test so the company could set up a truck-delivery system, Budd Axelrod read aloud from the test manual and quizzed his sons every night after dinner for a year.

When they went for their driver's tests, Kenny and Howard were the only ones in the family to pass on the first try.

In the stores, the two brothers dispense nutritional advice and take orders for custom blends from breeders, vets, and customers. They specially blend food for pets with dietary problems.

In addition to working in the stores, Jeanette still keeps a vigilant eye on progress in special education programs, particularly in the area of vocational training. When the company needed extra labor to cut out whole wheat dog biscuits, Mother's had the work done at a sheltered workshop for adults with Down's syndrome.

"I started this business so my sons would be okay if something happened to us," Jeanette says. "Now they don't really need me. Sometimes I think that with all my kids grown, *I'm* the one who really needs the business."

Recently, the family celebrated Howard's marriage to a woman he met in a special education class. After years of what his mother describes as "scrimping and brown-bagging his lunches," Howard got a ten-year mortgage and bought a small house.

"He did it all, and that was a real milestone," says Jeanette. "We call it the house that Mother built." [1]

## Seriously Handicapped?

I have a brother whose son was measured as a teen-aged boy and later as an adult to have the mental capacity of a small child. Indeed his perceptions and judgment are sharply limited, so much so that when he was a small child and I was graduate dean of a Napa Valley, California, college, I suggested that they might want to turn him over to a California State home for children in nearby Sonoma.

Charles answered, "Not a chance."

That was enough for me, but I thought at the time that he was overlooking a wonderful chance for special care, and they would have much more personal freedom. How foolish! I just did not know any better then, but I do now, for Charles and Doris taught me a badly-needed lesson. They centered their lives on that child—Doris, a registered nurse, and Charles, a competent college bindery foreman, with some help from Doris's mother.

In a few years that seriously handicapped child was playing cello solos, and occasionally he was at the organ or piano when no other musician was around. Music teachers informed them that Larry has perfect pitch. Now a man of forty-five, this nephew of ours can help cut and stack wood and do any number of errands around the house. But greatest of all is the precious and unmistakable symphony of love and satisfaction in that home, instead of the hollow emptiness they most certainly would have suffered if they had taken my inexperienced counsel and shallow concept of parental love.

Those forty-five years have on the one hand taught me the danger of placing limitations on genius, and on the other the richly rewarding experience of holding out fabulous expectations from love.

In the last decade or two, the development of programs for Down's syndrome youngsters has clearly shown that these handicapped people, once considered as hopeless and useless, can more often than not be educated to astonishing usefulness. Once called "Mongolian idiots," they are almost without exception gentle and loving individuals. Under warm and wise tutelage, they can be prepared to be among the most constructive handicapped people. And the earlier their special education is undertaken, the more and larger results will be realized.

So, warm parental responsiveness is as necessary and effective for the handicapped as for the genius. There are few management or industrial concepts in the home which the handicapped person cannot in some measure share.

# FOURTEEN

# PREPARING FOR EMPLOYMENT: HOME INDUSTRIES AND APPRENTICESHIPS

Y ou won't believe me, but we can't even find one totally prompt, dependable, and honest employee out of ten we interview." This owner of a chain of nursing homes was talking to us recently at an institutional dinner. Across the table a supermarket owner groaned, "Join the club!" I was talking that evening about balanced work-study programs at all levels in schools and colleges. Agreement was unanimous that work would both enrich achievement and strengthen character, but also unanimous was the certainty that this all should begin at home.

"It's high time we gave our children some responsibility," added the first speaker, "instead of indulging them at every turn." And he added that it would help if we would do much more to prepare our youngsters with enough occupational information and on-the-job experience to help them know how to find and hold a job.

*217*

## The Traditional Approach

Kathleen McCurdy, a leading Northwest parent educator has recently been writing and publishing in her newsletter, *Flex*, about her concern that our youth know enough to obtain bread-and-butter employment, whether or not they become professionals. In too many schools such instruction is limited to auto mechanics, home economics, woodworking, shorthand, and typing, and maybe a class in so-called life skills—how to fill out job applications and do job interviews.

A few decades ago, occupational education was largely ignored. "School" meant "academics," and concentration therefore was on developing the mind. Largely ignored was the historic principle of balance: When a person uses his hands as well as his head, his mental acuity is much sharper. This is one reason, for example, that students in California's Regional Occupational Programs produce the highest average scholarship in that state's high schools. The students go to school half a day and work half a day. In the old classical days—and still in some circles—Latin, philosophy, and classic literature were emphasized largely to the exclusion of physical work, which was considered unbecoming to a scholar.

On the other hand, in ancient Israel and other worthy civilizations down through the centuries, manual skills were of first importance. The ancient Hebrews, considered by many to be among the brightest people of all time, considered it a crime for a child to come out of school and into adulthood without sufficient manual skills to earn his own living. Reading was not in these cases the first priority. Unless he belonged to the ruling class or was to become a priest, too much book learning was often considered hazardous to success. And the outcome in today's schools generally supports this old fear.

Of course, it once was customary for boys to pursue their fathers' occupations. Except for royalty or other high caste families, it was not considered necessary or even wise to provide an academic education for girls; rather, they were expected to become skilled homemakers. Many women of royal lines eventually regretted their lack of these skills.

Princess Ileana, a great-granddaughter of England's Queen Victoria and Russia's Czar Alexander II and the last surviving child of Queen Marie of Romania, was once one of the world's most glamorous women. Yet she admitted sorrowfully to Jane Mayer of the *Wall Street Journal* of being reduced to living in a mobile home in Elwood City, Pennsylvania, as she spooned a few sardines packed in tomato sauce, "I never learned how to cook. I'm a very bad housekeeper, too. It was lacking in my education." [1] Her education was all intellectual and social. She was taught to "bow, bow, bow" to visiting dignitaries, and in turn expect them to kiss her hand—one "gracious" way to handicap an individual and leave her almost totally without practical skills.

## A Model for Learning Job Skills

Nowadays children are expected to be original and also to know from the time they are two or three years old what they want to be when they "grow up." But they are given very little help on exactly how to get there. Children who *have* figured out their life work often get their start by following in the footsteps of parents, relatives, or close friends who can help them. Getting close to these people is a logical place for many to start on their quest for employment.

A visit to the office or job or going on a service call can open a whole new range of understandings of how and why people work for a living. Otherwise children may tend to romanticize their parents' lives and discover to their surprise that drudgery, insecurity, and weariness may be their lot.

Along with a familiarity of their parents' and relatives' jobs, and well before they must think seriously about choosing careers for themselves, they should learn *how* to work. Certain skills are basic to all occupations and should be mastered at early ages when lifelong habits are being formed. These include thoughtfulness, promptness, thoroughness, orderliness, responsibility, efficiency, honesty, and common courtesy, among others. They are *learned* principles and skills as well as character traits, and they shine beautifully through when job application time comes.

Children can learn to pick up their toys when they start walking. By three or four, they can learn to clear the (unbreakable) dishes from the table, and by four or five to set it. By six or seven, they can do a worthy job dusting the furniture and sorting socks, shorts, and towels at laundry time. At eight or ten, most can reach an acceptable standard of dishwashing and begin to become efficient shoppers. Every chore is both a learning and business opportunity, building both principles and skills.

Unfortunately, most children are not allowed to help at early ages when they want to. Later, when they are eleven or twelve or into their teens, and parents think "It's about time you began to help around here," they have more urgent interests elsewhere.

Children need not only to learn *how* to work, but also opportunities to "try out" a number of occupations. They can start by assisting Grandpa or a neighbor in his shop, helping Dad work on the car, baby-sitting baby brother or a neighbor's child, or helping Mother or Dad balance the checkbook. They can learn a lot from a visit to the dentist, doctor, hairdresser, or an auto mechanic; or from watching a road crew, quizzing a piano tuner, observing the plumber, watching the mail man at close quarters, or even learning from the sales techniques of the Avon lady or the Fuller Brush man. This natural learning of the world around them is one of the best we can encourage, yet because we are not alert for the opportunities or because they become part of an educational institution so early, all too often we discourage.

From these impressionable experiences and successful chores at home, your child can advance to mowing neighbors' lawns, weeding their gardens, caring for their pets, delivering newspapers, bagging groceries, doing odd jobs, or any number of home industries listed or described in chapters 12 and 13. These give youngsters opportunities to learn the basics of job seeking, to develop self-confidence in dealing with people, to learn how to handle typical customer relations.

Volunteer work and apprenticeships offer other opportunities for career experience and a gradual transition into formal employment for pay. Candy stripers, assisting in nursing homes, and helping in political campaigns are several of hundreds of opportunities to learn about management and about government.

These kinds of experience are not only great in developing readiness for becoming a tradesman or mechanic, but also in making ready for college. Young men and women who have had such experiences with their fathers and others step out with much greater confidence, and young women who have apprenticed to good mothers feel confident of their homemaking skills.

In Madison, Wisconsin, fifteen-year-old Shane Alme gives us an unusually clear example of how children—or adults—can use apprenticeships and volunteer work to build a profession or trade and eventually to complement the family income. He not only continues his services to aged and disabled neighbors, but for several years has been an apprentice-volunteer at Channel 47, Madison, Wisconsin. He has made himself so valuable that he now is a full-time engineer at the station, declared by the manager to be one of the youngest licensed and employed master control operators in America "and among the best." For those who may have doubts about the demands of Shane's position, we received this job analysis from Ervin I. Vanags, Assistant Chief Engineer of WMSN-TV Channel 47, as part of his request to Federal authorities in behalf of Shane for a work permit:

> The duty of the Master Control Operator is primarily to monitor the actual off-air signal of the television station. This consists of the following:
>
> 1. Following the order of the traffic log to air both programs and commercial announcements as they have been listed.
> 2. To verify that the listings of the log have been aired as scheduled and check off each event as it is aired.
> 3. To note any deviations from the log and list them in the Discrepancy Report.

4. To monitor the electrical parameters of both the video and audio signal and make certain that it meets Federal Communications Commission standards for transmitted television signals.

5. To take transmitter readings to verify that the signal power of the aural and visual signals are within FCC limits, and also monitor other transmitting parameters to check the performance of the transmitter.

6. To pull tapes, load video tape recorders, sequence tapes, and run the master control switching system to air programs and commercials.

For all the value of a formal education and college degrees, employers have come more and more to make clear that experience may be more valuable than a degree. Children who have had opportunities to develop good work habits and have acquired some experience in their chosen fields, who understand something of economic principles and interpersonal relations, are the young men and women who will get the jobs. These seldom if ever become burdens to society.

## German Vocational Education

Steve Hamilton, a Cornell University professor of human development and family studies and colleague of Urie Bronfenbrenner, whom we often quote, has recently completed a highly documented and very well informed book on *Apprenticeship for Adulthood: Preparing Youth for the Future*—one that every educator and parent should carefully read.[2] He contrasts German and American vocational education and shows with remarkable clarity how apprenticeship programs in Germany give the student an early sense of security. They are often preferred to college entrance courses, although students can return to *Realschule* (technical middle school) to earn the *Arbitur* (college entrance certificate). Their *Berufsschule* (the part-time vocational school which apprentices attend) generally starts earlier than America's—from ages fifteen to nineteen—finishing about the time American students start actual apprenticeships, which is *after* they graduate from high school.

We strongly agree with Dr. Hamilton's conclusion that "American schools isolate youth from adults and from workplaces and other community settings." He adds, "Weak links between school and work, combined with initial confinement to the secondary labor market, cloud young people's futures." In other words, we need to get our youth much earlier into practical apprenticeship training which provides "a stronger dose of planned work experience." He states flatly that "American schools . . . force youth to wait too long for the promised rewards and obscure for them the relation between what they are doing now and what they will be doing in the future."

The German *Berufsschulen* are designed to supplement apprenticeships in contrast with the American vocational schools which are generally developed to replace the apprenticeship. Furthermore, the German programs range from training for skilled mechanics to mid- and upper-level business careers. Open to the German youth are not only the *Industriekaufleute*—apprenticeships in industrial firms—but there are also *Kaufleute* in banking, real estate, wholesale and retail trade, insurance, advertising, and other separate apprentice training fields. Their *mentors* are skilled craftsmen with them constantly. This teacher-student symphony we have found to be crucial in similar programs which we developed in Japan, Manila, and here in the United States.

Dr. Hamilton also supports our earlier reference to the high discipline and achievement of the California ROP's, in noting that such work experience needs (and in the ROP's, receives) "increased academic rigor." And in different words, yet in clear and pointed terms, he stresses the urgency to develop in American youngsters the central philosophy of this book—the determination to sacrifice present pleasures for future benefits. Instead of preparing them for the primary or adult labor market, we frustrate them by dangling only the low-pay secondary or youth labor market before them. Says Hamilton:

Youth facing poverty and discrimination are particularly prone to
doubt that they can improve their future prospects materially by
working hard in school and behaving responsibly or, conversely,
that they place themselves at substantially greater risk of adult
distress by failing in school and by engaging in self-destructive
and socially irresponsible behavior [drugs, sex, delinquency, violence, etc]. They see themselves as headed for dead-end jobs,
unemployment, and welfare regardless of what they do. 'Why not
get what pleasure you can?' they ask themselves. 'Why postpone
gratification that may never come again?' The probable returns
for avoiding self-destructive behavior and working hard in school
do not appear to them sufficient to justify abstinence, responsibility, diligence, and possible alienation from peers.[3]

By teaching apprentices early the necessary knowledge, skills, and
attitudes, the German *Berufsschulen* build into their youth a sense
of responsibility and the assurance that theirs is a direct route to a
satisfying adult career.

We do not want to convey the idea here that America is totally
indifferent to apprenticeships, for there are many public, private,
and parochial ones which operate. One of the more prominent of
these is the Gothard A.T.I.A. program which even advocates apprenticeships for medicine and law.[4]

Americans have the resources both in money and teaching talent (from both schools and industry). All they lack is the system
and the discipline. The system is available, given the highly-success-
ful German example. Discipline, we have found, comes quickly
once the students clearly see the system's common sense and its
certain rewards. In this sense, we believe that early apprenticeships
provide one of the most certain routes to setting aside the temptations of present gratification as they are given a clearer and more
attractive view of future benefits.

# FIFTEEN

# SOMETHING FOR SINGLE PARENTS, TOO

J ust as Thomas Edison has been a historic model of home educated boys, who gained a richer education by going into business with the encouragement of his mother, so Sarah Josepha Hale
was a queenly example a hundred years ago for today's single
moms—who are among our most worthy treasures. Sarah didn't
let her singleness keep her from writing "Mary Had a Little Lamb"
or persuading Abraham Lincoln to declare Thanksgiving a national holiday. We tell her story here because it seems to have
nearly all the elements and obstacles experienced and faced by
modern single mothers. Perhaps the principal difference in those
days was the status of women who often enjoyed less respect than
we now accord a household pet.

Despite her almost complete lack of formal schooling until she
was a mother, Sarah was considered one of the nineteenth
century's greatest crusaders. Certainly she was one of America's
most influential professional women. It was said that she could
drive a hard business bargain, yet be a perfect lady who could weep
over a faded violet. Although her name was known across the nation for one of its most widely memorized poems, she was penni-

less, the bereaved mother of five young children. She waited until 1828, six years a widow, before she entered public life at age forty.

Taught at home by her brother, Horatio, during his vacations from college, she became an avid scholar without any formal schooling and at twenty-five married lawyer David Hale, one of the catches of the age. David was fascinated with her extraordinary beauty and the completeness of her mind. She returned her husband's admiration, but her fascination was with writing—which she indulged whenever she had a spare moment from her brood. She and her husband reveled in two planned hours of daily study—French, Latin, botany, geology, and world history—until 1822 when pneumonia suddenly robbed her of him. The young widow's oldest child was nine, and Sarah was eight and a half months pregnant with her fifth.

Untrained as a wage earner or business woman, she scraped out a bare existence. She tried setting up a millinery shop, but she failed. Knowing that you learn to write by writing, she kept at it every spare moment, and by 1827 published *Northwood, A Tale of New England,* a best seller about slavery which was published more than twenty years before *Uncle Tom's Cabin.* That success catapulted her to editorial prominence, and she became editor of *Ladies Magazine*—a daring adventure in those days, considering the male dominance of the publishing industry. Yet Sarah told her readers she wasn't interested in fame, but "only to support and educate my five children."

Ridiculed, scoffed, and harassed by the male frontier, she thought her break was at hand when, for lack of money, construction of the Bunker Hill Monument was stopped at a height of forty feet. Yet when she suggested that American women might help raise funds, newspapers laughed. Nevertheless, in those days when women controlled little or no money, gently persuasive Sarah soon had American women knitting, crocheting, putting up jellies and jams, and otherwise manually earning what then was an unearthly goal of thirty thousand dollars.

She wooed rich patronesses by printing their names in a special publication, *The Monument,* which she published only for that purpose. Sarah's efforts culminated in a fair at Boston's Quincy Hall where the accumulated products of women's hands were sold, and in a week, to male consternation and newspaper blushes, she presented the Monument Association with thirty thousand dollars.

Even though she was reared as a gentlewoman, Sarah Hale became a champion of the work ethic. She wrote in her magazine that the poor needed work, not charity. Her causes eventually embraced an astonishing variety of needs—from Seaman's Aid Society and the Merchant Marine Library to the first industrial school for girls and America's first day nursery. She had a special concern for infants whose mothers couldn't or wouldn't care for them, and was a determined foe of sweatshops and child labor.

Eventually Sarah became editor of *Godey's Lady's Book* which was a combination of Louis Godey's *Lady's Book* and the *Ladies Magazine.* Before she wrote her last editorial at age ninety, she campaigned for ladies' high schools, more women doctors, women clerks, and was a key initiator and supporter of Vassar College. She had encouraged any kind of invention—double boilers, rotary egg beaters, crude washing machines—that would lighten women's burdens. She had investigated and approved dozens of inventions from the sanitation of mattresses to the respectability and security of steam railroads; had advocated at least a bath a week and opposed tight corsets and airless bedrooms.

An American beauty who for more than ninety years maintained an utter simplicity—she demurely wore black and a widow's cap—Sarah Josepha Buell Hale outwalked her grandchildren almost to her dying day. Because of her selfless peace and care of her body, it was said that her pink-and-white complexion was unlined, her long-lashed hazel eyes needed no glasses, and her brown curls were still glossy. Sarah kept her mind where it belonged—on her children and on others who were in need. A single woman.[1]

If you are a single parent or are a friend of a single parent who is in need of an industry at home, look down the lists and through the stories in chapters 10 and 11 with that person in mind. At least half or three-quarters of the businesses would accommodate singles' needs if handled with wisdom, persistence, and courage. Take as an example, running garage sales. These take little capital or overhead, get you out of the house, and can be profitable with a little care. We pass on a few suggestions from Harry Foster who is an accountant in Stuart, Florida. While he limits his remarks primarily to garage sales, we hope that his way of going about such a project will be something of a model for single parents for other projects as well, especially in view of the model of Sarah Hale. And the ideas here are certainly suitable for *any* garage sale whether operated by singles or marrieds.

Mr. Foster suggests that you might encourage other singles by inviting them to work with you. This doesn't proscribe married men or women, but it can be an outreach to other singles. It also gives them an opportunity to divest themselves of unwanted or unneeded items that otherwise might be difficult, since most singles don't have as much to sell as a typical family.

His ideas involve a systematic procedure which should be applied in principle to any home industry:

- Determine with whom you will share your project, if any.

- Pick your date.

- Select your site, remembering visibility, traffic flow, and parking availability.

- Allow yourself at least three or four weeks to prepare.

- Check local laws. They may demand permits or prohibit sales.

- Investigate ordinances regarding advertising.

- Visit other garage sales and learn techniques first hand.

- Study layout, tagging, pricing, advertising.

- Note how different items sell.

- If a joint sale, agree on split of profits beforehand. He says you may divide equally, no matter whose stuff is sold; use different colored price tags for different participants and remove and record them when items are sold, and have each person record his own sales in a ledger.

- Gather your merchandise, carefully examining every nook and cranny; even you may be surprised at what you have.

- Make your display presentable, waxing and polishing your tables, polishing silverware, sharpening knives, cleaning away grease from garage or automobile items.

- Price your items at an attractive level, but leave room for that fascinating exercise of bargaining, so that customers can go home to brag about the deal they made.

- Finally, be honest.[2]

Harry Foster doesn't bypass advertising. He considers this crucial. He urges you to use not only the typical highway signs and bulletin board cards, but develop neat, well-versed newspaper ads, and don't forget radio stations. Some of them, we might note, will do this for you as a public service if you specify that the income is for some charitable purpose.

And finally don't forget to get to the bank for some change. Many single and married folks, particularly women, do very well running garage sales for other families. Dorothy found great relief in obtaining the expert garage sale services of her dear friend (but not a relative) Marceil Moore of Berrien Springs, Michigan. Judy Kramer and Audrey De Young, two Washington, D.C., housewives reportedly often gross from three thousand to ten thousand dollars annually, which as Harry Foster would say is "not bad for a day's work."

# SIXTEEN

# CONSIDERING THE LAW'S DEMANDS

S ome of you who read this book will remember a story which came out of Virginia eight or ten years ago. It was about a young lady whose name, I believe, was Christine. Christine kept goats and sold their milk for at least part of her living. But one day some official arranged to have a new statute placed on the books which required expensive sterilization and cooling equipment common these days to large dairies. She knew she had to find a way around the law or go out of business.

She decided to continue to sell milk until the authorities stopped her. She hadn't reckoned with another, larger goat farmer who had complied with the new state regulations at great expense and was now determined that Christine would, too. So he had her brought into court.

The judge heard her kindly and let her go free. But her competitor insisted that the State of Virginia appeal the case, and on appeal, she lost.

Next, her creative and determined brain invented the idea of "Rent-a-goat." This way, theoretically, she was no longer running a dairy. But her nemesis again reported her, again lost in the first court, but won against her again on appeal.

Now desperate, she one day spotted some goat manure. She would sell goat manure for two or three dollars a bag, and whoever wanted any milk, could have it free. The last we talked with her, Christine was still selling composted goat manure, and it wasn't surprising how many also wanted free milk.

Whatever else we tell you in this chapter, we encourage you to have the courage of your convictions. We will not encourage you to break a law, but we may suggest that you find your common sense way around it as long as you don't violate the law's spirit.

Although we have emphasized home industries for more than forty years, it wasn't until the early 1970s that we began to hear regularly from families who asked for information on home businesses. Barbara Little wrote one of these letters from Vancouver, Washington, in September, 1983. We use it here because it brought up many of the typical questions and doubts. She began by asking us to "open it up to readers of [*The Moore Report*] in the letter column," then continued:

> We would like to start a cottage industry and are especially interested in doing something in the area of food. What holds us back is meeting State Health Regulations. Years ago when I considered doing this I sent for information from the State Health Department. There are a lot of requirements that would be very difficult and/or expensive to meet. I also believe that everyone preparing food to sell needs to have a food-handler's license. It is my understanding that only people sixteen years and older can obtain a license of this nature, thus eliminating our children from helping.
>
> So my question: How are families doing it? Am I misinterpreting the state regulations? Are families meeting these requirements, or are they ignoring the legal guidelines? We admire families who are selling sandwiches, bread, muffins, etc. But how do they do it? . . .

First, we must face the fact that in some communities and states there is a great deal of confusion about home industries, with labor unions, local businesses, and other vested interests and departments of health and safety vying for control at the state and local legislative and statutory levels. You must not be fearful of these operators and officials, but instead work positively with them on a course of truth, and stay with it until homes receive fair treatment while accommodating sound laws of health and safety. Yet we believe that there has been much more openness among state and local officials in the last few years.

As we pointed out earlier, expectations for home industries are mounting, in substantial part because it allows women to be home with their children. Yet there are basic considerations which are unlikely to change. Among these are well-founded fears that disease is easily spread in food-related industries by unclean hands and unsanitary facilities. Another is the certainty that a person should demonstrate a reasonable maturity in any institutional setting before he is put in charge of a machine which may risk life or limb.

Barbara asks how families are meeting these obstacles. We know of families who go down the center of the road with the law, usually carrying on a substantial commercial operation and doing a fairly broad job of marketing. Then there are other families who operate on a very small, informal basis, letting people know that they are baking bread or cookies or muffins. Often their foods are sampled at a charity or church bake sale and are so delicious that they soon find that they have a number of regular customers. Some health departments would frown on such a practice; others turn their heads, reasoning, as one official put it, "Who would ever want to stop a bake sale? Why, that is a part of Americana!"

Church and community pot-luck dinners and benefit suppers, by Kiwanis, Rotary, Elks and other service clubs, have operated for many years without notable interference from state or town officials. Women's organizations often serve benefit meals. One time not long ago we attended a spaghetti dinner put on by a men's club, with the men cooking on the spot. So, before we discuss our legal obligations, it is only reasonable to suggest that there are exceptions. Usually when little children bake, they are viewed as delightful and, certainly, acceptable entrepreneurs. Common sense must reign. It is the genuine commercial operation that appears to be the target of most of these statutes.

The same applies generally to safety regulations. The rules against use of power machinery by children under sixteen usually apply to institutions. Parents can pretty much do as they please in sharing such tools with their own children, but they had better be careful about their use by anyone else, regardless of age, lest they open themselves for major legal tangles.

Bertha Goettemoeller, who has written frequently along these lines for home educators, says it simply: "There are . . . legal questions to pursue such as zoning laws, licensing, and state and federal regulations. City Hall, your local Chamber of Commerce, and county officials are possible sources of help on these points. At any rate, don't depend on hearsay. You need to know the correct procedures for *your area*." [1]

Some successful home business people point out that there is no particular virtue in probing too deeply into gray areas, such as children baking bread for their neighbors. We counsel along the lines of Mrs. Goettemoeller, yet we believe that common sense will solve a lot of these problems, especially with a local home or church clientele.

The rigid quality of many labor statutes may be attributed as much to vested pressures by labor unions as to health and safety. Only very recently, late in 1988, the U. S. Department of Labor lifted a forty-five-year-old ban on manufacturing gloves, buttons, buckles, embroidery, handkerchiefs, and jewelry at home. However, there is still a stop on making women's clothes commercially there. John Goodman of the National Center for Policy Analysis believes that "The right to engage in home-based work will probably be the single most important women's issue of the next decade." This is of course a labor union "No-no." The AFL-CIO is against even home-based clerical work because it "inhibits union organizing." An excellent source for such information is the National Center for Privatization. [2]

Jan Fletcher and Jane Williams also insist in "Editor's notes" in the *Home Business Advisor* that heavily-funded political action committees (PACs) of the labor unions constitute home industry's most formidable opponents. [3] They point out that these PACs work hard to persuade legislators that poor women are tied to their computers producing piece work (claims processing, for example) and getting paid slave wages with no benefits because they are classified as "independent contractors." Mrs. Fletcher and Mrs. Williams note the fallacy of this argument, but warn also that we must take care that we don't make our home industries pink-collar ghettos.

The laborer is worthy of his hire—a principle we should bear deeply in mind in dealing with all, but particularly with women and children, in view of their vulnerability. We must also be alert to legislation which affects our rights in our homes, just as some of us have been working in unity and with signal success in legislatures and courts across America, Canada, Australia, New Zealand, and elsewhere overseas to protect parental rights in the education of their children.

We mention unity, for in every major effort at reform and community and family interests, sooner or later the primary problem is not the public official or labor organizer or other enemy. Rather the most invidious and insidious (check those words in your dictionary) tend to be individuals or groups *within* the movements which have their own agendas to develop their own constituencies, whatever their motives. This is born out in both sides of the abortion controversy, the anti-pornography movement, and others. The home deserves your best, and families will only be fully protected in the face of ambitious states and other industries when they close ranks and present the truths and high motives and accomplishments of home industries as they truly deserve.

# EPILOGUE

Y ou will have the gratitude and praise of your children and of future societies if you build up a self-starting citizenry who are more interested in developing financial independence and manual skills as they are in being entertained.

# APPENDIX

# RESOURCES

The following books and other sources are listed alphabetically to ensure that we do not give the impression that we are placing them in any particular category, lest you be disappointed because any one of them does not comprehensively fulfill your expectations for your area of interest. We do not necessarily recommend these books nor take the responsibility for their accuracy or effectiveness, but only list them as a service to you and to show the wide variety of sources available. We also invite your attention to highly-selected books mentioned in various chapters of this book.

Becker, Benjamin M., and Fred A. Tillman. *The Family Owned Business.* Commerce Clearing House, Inc., Chicago, 1973.

Belliston, Larry, and Kurt Hanks. *Extra Cash for Kids.* Wolgemuth and Hyatt, Brentwood, TN, 1982.

Burkett, Larry. *Answers to Your Family's Financial Questions.* Focus on the Family Publishing, Pomona, CA, 1987.

——— *The Complete Financial Guide for Young Couples.* Victor Books, Wheaton, IL, 1989.

——— *Debt-Free Living.* Moody Press, Chicago, 1989.

———— *Get a Grip on Your Money.* Two volumes: Student text and teacher's guide for senior high. Focus on the Family Publishing, Pomona, CA, 1990.

———— *Surviving the Money Jungle.* Two volumes: Student text and teacher's guide for junior high. Focus on the Family Publishing, Pomona, CA, 1990.

———— *What Husbands Wish Their Wives Knew About Money.* Victor Press, Wheaton, IL, 1977/1989.

———— *What the Bible Says about Money.* Wolgemuth & Hyatt, Brentwood, TN, 1989.

———— *Your Finances in Changing Times.* Moody Press, Chicago, 1975.

Gibson, Mary Bass. *The Family Circle Book of Careers at Home.* Cowles Book Co., Inc., Chicago, 1971.

Hamilton, Stephen F. *Apprenticeships for Adulthood: Preparing Youth for the Future.* Macmillan, New York, 1990.

Kahm, H.S. *101 Businesses You Can Start and Run with Less Than $1,000.* Parker Publishing Co., West Nyack, NY, 1968.

Kern, Coralee, and Tammara Wolfgram. *Planning Your Own Home Business.* National Textbook Company, 1986.

Kishel, Gregory, and Patricia Gunter-Kishel. *Dollars on Your Doorstep.* John Wiley and Sons, Inc., New York, 1984.

McCullough, Bonnie R. *Bonnie's Household Organizer.* St. Martin's Press, New York, 1981.

McCullough, Bonnie R., and Susan W. Monson. *401 Ways to Get Your Kids to Work at Home.* St. Martin's Press, New York, 1981.

Moore, Raymond. *Home Made Health.* Word Books, Irving, TX, 1989.

Moore, Raymond, and Dorothy Moore. *Home-Grown Kids.* Word Books, Irving, TX, 1984.

———— ———— *Home School Burnout: What It Is, What Causes It, &
How to Cure It.* Wolgemuth & Hyatt, Brentwood, TN, 1988.

———— ———— *Homebuilt Discipline.* Thomas Nelson, Nashville, TN,
1987.

———— ———— *Homespun Schools.* Word Books, Irving, TX, 1987.

Steinhoff, Dan. *Small Business Management Fundamentals.* McGraw-
Hill, New York, 1982.

Young, Pam, and Peggy Jones. *Sidetracked Home Executives.* Warner
Books, Inc., New York, 1981.

🐦 🐦 🐦

The magazine, *Selling Direct,* also has many ideas for successful
home businesses: 6255 Barfield Road, Atlanta, GA 30328.

Also the newsletter, "Family-Owned Businesses," 1120 Vermont
Ave., NW Suite 1200, Washington, D.C., 20005. (A publication
of *Business Week*), phone (202) 463-1789.

# NOTES

## Chapter 2: How to Coach Young Financiers

1. Larry Burkett, *The Complete Financial Guide for Young Couples* (Wheaton, IL: Victor Books, 1989). For more information on Larry Burkett books and financial manuals, see your bookstore or send a SASE to: Money Matters, P.O. Box 100, Gainesville, GA 30503. For orders only, telephone (800) 722-1976.

## Chapter 3: Values: How Much Are You Worth?

1. Urie Bronfenbrenner, *Two Worlds of Childhood* (New York: Simon and Schuster, 1970).

2. Raymond and Dorothy Moore *Home Grown Kids,* (Irving, TX: Word Books, 1984).

3. Joanne Kaufman, *Wall Street Journal,* "A Maitre d' with the Mostest," February 6, 1990, A-20.

4. Bronfenbrenner, 66.

5. For verification of this, read any of several well-documented books by the Moores listed in the appendix. For a book list or other information, send a SASE to Moore Foundation, Box 1, Camas, WA 98607.

6. David Quine, "The Intellectual Development of Home Taught Children," an unpublished paper done in connection with research at the University of Oklahoma, 1987.

## Chapter 4: The Wasteful Generation

1. For carefully-documented, practical hints along these lines, read the authors' book, *Home Made Health,* available from the Moore Foundation, Box 1, Camas, WA 98607 or your local bookstore.

2. Tufts University Diet & Nutrition Letter, Vol. 7, No. 9, November 1989.

3. We are indebted in part for this material on waste reduction to the Prince William County. Reprinted with permission from the Prince William County, VA Department of Public Works, December 1989.

## Chapter 5: Recycling: Happily Making New Out of Old

1. Much of this chapter offers information gleaned from publications of the Prince William County Solid Waste Division and is reprinted with permission from the Prince William County, VA, Department of Public Works.

## Chapter 6: They Who Serve: The Twice Blessed

1. For simple and scientific guidance along these lines, see the *American Red Cross Handbook,* obtainable from your local librarian or health department.

## Chapter 7: Organization: Just a Little Bit at a Time

1. To avoid embarrassment we have changed the actual names in this true story.

2. Raymond and Dorothy Moore, *Homebuilt Disciple,* (Nashville, TN: Thomas Nelson, 1987).

3. Steven N. Blair, *Newsweek,* November 13, 1989.

4. Shellee Nunley, "The Art of Organization," *The Desert Sun,* Palm Springs, CA, March 3, 1990, pages H1 and H7.

5. L. W. Warren and J. Ostrom, "Pack rats: world-class savers." *Psychology Today,* Vol. 22, April 1988, 58–62.

6. Perry Buffington, Ph.D., "Store It Away," *Sky*, February 1990, 71–74.

## Chapter 9: The C-I Magic: Why Cottage Industries Are Special

1. These and other statistics are also reported by *Family Policy*, a journal of The Family Research Council of America, Washington, D.C., November–December 1988.

2. *U.S. News and World Report*, December 26, 1989, 120.

## Chapter 10: How Others Do It

1. Raymond and Dorothy Moore, *Home Style Teaching* (Irving, TX: Word Books, 1984). This collection of simple but creative ideas for sound teaching has been widely used by teachers in public, private, parochial, and home schools.

2. Raymond and Dorothy Moore, *Home School Burnout*, (Brentwood, TN: Wolgemuth & Hyatt, 1988).

3. Vicki Livingstone, ed. *Chea News*, as reported by the Canadian Home Education Association of British Columbia.

4. American Rabbit Breeders Association, Box 426, Bloomington, IL 61702.

5. Families for Home Education, October 1986, and other regular columns on home industries. Families for Home Education is the former name of a newsletter of an organization of the same name. The newsletter is now called Heart of America Report, Sara Lee Rhoads, editor; Sibley, MO.

6. For easily-read, but thoroughly-documented information on how children develop, see the books by Raymond and Dorothy Moore: *Better Late Than Early*, Readers Digest Press, 1975, now published by the Moore Foundation, Box 1 Camas, WA 98607, or *Home Grown Kids*, (Irving, TX: Word Books, 1980), available from the Moore Foundation or your local book store. A highly-documented book designed for scholars is the

Moore's *School Can Wait*, formerly published by a university press, but now distributed by the Moore Foundation.

7. *Home Business Advisor*, (Fayetteville, NC: NextStep Publications, July 1987).

8. Ron Duncan, *Home School Journal*, formerly published by Warren Rushton and others in Columbus, NE.

9. In *Child's Play*, the newsletter of the Canadian Alliance of Homeschoolers, reporting on By Our Kids, Ltd. of 8154 Alfalfa, Longmont, CO 80501.

10. Mark and Laurie Sleeper, *Home Sweet Home*, No. 1, Fall 1989, P.O. Box 1254, Milton, WA 98354.

## Chapter 13: When the Handicapped Become Assets

1. For information on the pet foods or her program, write to Jeanette Axelrod at: Mother's, 727 Montgomery Avenue, Narberth, PA 19072. This story was reported in the *Family Circle Magazine*, February 1971. Used by permission.

## Chapter 14: Preparing for Employment: Home Industries and Apprenticeships

1. Jane Mayer, *Wall Street Journal*, Vol. CXXII, No.6, January 23, 1990.

2. Steve Hamilton, *Apprenticeship for Adulthood: Preparing Youth for the Future*, (The Free Press [Macmillan], 1990).

3. Ibid.

4. We suggest that you send a SASE to: Apprenticeship Information, Box 1, Oakbrook, IL 60521.

## Chapter 15: Something for Single Parents, Too

1. For more on Sarah Hale, read *The Lady of Godey's* by Ruth E. Finley, (Philadelphia, PA: J. B. Lippincott Co., 1931). Her story is also digested in *Secrets of Successful Living, Book Six*, (Pleasantville, NY: *Reader's Digest*, 10570).

2. Harry H. Foster, "Maximizing Your Garage Sale," *Christian Single,* (Nashville, TN: June 1987).

## Chapter 16: Considering the Law's Demands

1. Bertha Goettemoeller, "Cottage Industries," *Families for Home Education,* October 1986. 1525 West Lexington, Independence, MO 64052.

2. One of our sources for this information is the National Center for Privatization's monthly newsletter, *Private Solutions,* Vol. X, Number 5, May 1989, 2.

3. *Home Business Advisor,* Vol. 1, Number 1, July 1987, NextStep Publications, P.O. Box 41108, Fayetteville, NC 28309.

# SUBJECT INDEX

# ABOUT THE AUTHORS

R aymond and Dorothy Moore have been working together for more than fifty years. Dorothy credits Raymond with initiative and courage, but he trumpets her wisdom and boasts that she is "the best management head in the business." For nearly all of this time, Raymond has been fishing schools and colleges out of debt and consulting around the world on balanced work-study programs.

The Moores have authored several books including *Home Made Health* (Word Books, Irving, TX, 1989); *Home School Burnout: What It Is, What Causes It, & How to Cure It* (Wolgemuth & Hyatt, Publishers, Inc., Brentwood, TN, 1988); *Home-Grown Kids* (Word Books, Irving, TX, 1984); *Homebuilt Discipline* (Thomas Nelson, Nashville, TN, 1987); and *Homespun Schools* (Word Books, Irving, TX, 1987).

Honored by presidents and princes, universities and families across the land, the Moores have enjoyed more than three thousand interviews ranging from *Time,* "Today," "Donahue," "Ophra Winfrey," *Wall Street Journal,* and "Focus on the Family" to the all Australia TV program "Monday Conference" and others across the world. With Dorothy's mastery of remedial reading and Dr. Moore's experience as school superintendent, college and U.S. Office of Education official, the duo fathered and mothered the modern highly-productive home school renaissance at an age many educators retire. Together they have authored or contributed to more than sixty books and monographs and countless articles.

The typeface for the text of this book is *Baskerville*. It's creator, John Baskerville (1706-1775), broke with tradition to reflect in his type the rounder, yet more sharply cut lettering of eighteenth-century stone inscriptions and copy books. The type foreshadows modern design in such novel characteristics as the increase in contrast between thick and thin strokes and the shifting of stress from the diagonal to the vertical strokes. Realizing that this new style of letter would be most effective if cleanly printed on smooth paper with genuinely black ink, he built his own presses, developed a method of hot pressing the printed sheet to a smooth, glossy finish, and experimented with special inks. However, Baskerville did not enter into general commercial use in England until 1923.

*Substantive Editing:*
Michael S. Hyatt

*Copy Editing:*
Cynthia Tripp

*Cover Design:*
Steve Diggs & Friends
Nashville, Tennessee

*Page Composition:*
Xerox Ventura Publisher
Printware 720 IQ Laser Printer

*Printing and Binding:*
Maple-Vail Book Manufacturing Group
York, Pennsylvania

*Cover Printing:*
Strine Printing Company
York, Pennsylvania